TAKE MASSIVE ACTION

TAKE MASSIVE ACTION

TOWARD YOUR DREAMS

CHRISTINA KUMAR

NEW DEGREE PRESS
COPYRIGHT © 2021 CHRISTINA KUMAR
All rights reserved.
TAKE MASSIVE ACTION
Toward Your Dreams

ISBN	978-1-63730-668-0	*Paperback*
	978-1-63730-757-1	*Kindle Ebook*
	979-8-88504-046-4	*Ebook*

To the person who needs to hear this,
You can do it.

CONTENTS

| | INTRODUCTION | 9 |

PART 1.	**THE POWER OF THE START**	**15**
CHAPTER 1.	START NOW	17
CHAPTER 2.	THE POWER OF MOMENTUM	31
CHAPTER 3.	WHY START AT THIS MOMENT?	47

PART 2.	**THE PRINCIPLES OF ACTION**	**57**
CHAPTER 4.	IMPORTANCE OF BOLDNESS	59
CHAPTER 5.	TAKE SMART RISKS	75
CHAPTER 6.	KEEP CREATING	91
CHAPTER 7.	TRYING THINGS IN A SHORT PERIOD OF TIME	103
CHAPTER 8.	RAPID LEARNERS	113
CHAPTER 9.	TEACHERS AND MENTORS	121

PART 3.	**ACTION-TO-MOMENTUM MINDSET**	**133**
CHAPTER 10.	STARTING YOUR IDEA	135
CHAPTER 11.	HOW TO DEVELOP AN ACTION-TO-MOMENTUM MINDSET	147
CHAPTER 12.	AMBITIOUS APTITUDE	159

	EPILOGUE	169
	ACKNOWLEDGMENTS	173
	APPENDIX	175

INTRODUCTION

"Create a definite plan for carrying out your desire and begin at once, whether you are ready or not, to put this plan into action." (Action, n.d.)

—NAPOLEON HILL

Solving our own problems. Is that possible? Yes. Time and time again, individuals conquer their seemingly insurmountable problems and make a success out of doing so. The examples are infinite, but what you don't hear about is the backstory of these examples, many of which include only a single person with a dream.

Take this once-relatively unknown glassblowing artist whose company is now a household name. Jim McKelvey, cofounder of Square, Inc., didn't come from great wealth or have meaningful connections in the industry he first set out to conquer. Yet Square now has a valuation of over one hundred billion dollars and Jim is on the *Forbes'* billionaires list. I had the honor of speaking with him and learned he is a humble person interested in helping others. At first, he was a simple glassblowing artist who had lost a major sale because he couldn't take a credit card payment since it had high fees.

However, he took the initiative to call a friend. A friend he once was the boss of, but now was an equal. That friend was Jack Dorsey, the current CEO of both Square, Inc. and Twitter. Jack Dorsey at the time had been fired from Twitter, so they decided to build a financial services and digital payments company without having any experience in the industry. Jim could have waited around looking for someone else to solve his problem, but he realized the power of taking action that builds the momentum needed to solve a problem. And that changed history!

I wondered if this approach in taking simple actions to build momentum, as Jim did, was unique or if it was something that all of us could learn from. What I have found has transformed the way I see building momentum forever.

Studies show that more than half of US workers are not happy and are not satisfied with their work (Kelly, 2019). Reasons include not being engaged or connected to their work and also not feeling heard. This is alarming. Since the United States sets the standard for the rest of the world, we definitely need to do more to mitigate this situation. While we often look to others such as our bosses for guidance, now is the time to take a different approach to actually change the situation at hand. We have to look at the people who have inspired us with their leaps of faith and were able to create their own path as our guiding light.

This is what I did, and it has greatly impacted my own life. I had signed up to do a fifty-four-hour business competition, which was powered by Google for Entrepreneurs called Startup Weekend. The event had started on Friday, November 13, 2015, in a new co-working space in California. This was the first time I had ever heard about an event like this, and I was very curious. At that time, I had begun working in a new position I did not like and knew wasn't for me. I had always had a love for business and entrepreneurship, so I thought this was a good opportunity to get involved in the entrepreneurial community and see what happens.

The pitch practice was an event before the competition that gave us a chance to practice our pitch and get feedback from peers and coaches before the competition began. This was a nerve-racking prospect, and although I was somewhat apprehensive, I still attended. I knew this was great practice to get before the competition. I was able to meet new people and get a feel for where things may lead. People from all over California attended the event. I talked to some interesting people and learned about new ideas and concepts.

Never did I imagine what was about to occur!

I looked around the room, and it was packed. I was nervous at the last-minute changes taking place before our presentations. The judges were there, and we had to do our best. The Internet gave out earlier, and I had rushed to a nearby boba shop to finish our presentation while my team practiced our speech. Standing in line to go next for our presentation, we were ready. We were finally going to pitch our service, a service that gave users the ability to leave a video message right after a call was missed instead of the usual voicemail option.

Things were going off to a good start…until our laptop wasn't connecting to the monitor! A competing team member came up and helped us with this technical issue. That was a relief. After the presentation, all we had to do was wait.

Then it happened.

The announcer called my team's name as the winner.

As I heard my team's name called out by the announcer stating that we had won, I looked around and grinned at one of my teammates. I walked up on stage, and my team was right behind me in shock. I hadn't known for a fact that we were going to win but, at that moment, I was in alignment. That elusive feeling we get when we know something is meant to be.

After this win, I knew I would write a book about the experience. I knew the information I gathered throughout this experience would come in handy as I learned a lot in a short amount of time. Most importantly, I learned that the best wins come from the most action. Everyone thinks you have to wait for the right opportunity, but I believe in another approach: take action. Build momentum. Grow. And generate the right timing even if you are unsure of the results.

I feel compelled to write about this because I too had thought that you have to wait for the right timing, but then I learned, in an eye-opening way, how this is not accurate. I started to research and talk to those I admire, many of them who are at the top of their fields, and I learned very important strategies that changed the views I had been programmed with.

I had faced multiple fears all at once.

I had to create a company with total strangers. Most importantly, I had to take part in public speaking. I also had to communicate like my life depended on it and look the other way at any criticisms that may have come up. Chaos and anxiety were everywhere, but I knew my love of business and entrepreneurship outweighed the fear of the unknown, and I took action. Massive action. As a result, we won first place. This had fast-tracked everything, lowered my fear of public speaking, and I had learned about how to work better in teams. It also prepared me for obstacles and gave me the knowledge I needed to proceed in business. Primarily, it taught me the power of taking action.

Take Massive Action: Toward Your Dreams

Take Massive Action: Toward Your Dreams takes us through a journey of success and gaining the confidence needed to obtain it. It navigates us through the real-life stories of extraordinary individuals who were once everyday people. These select individuals were able to apply the wisdom they needed to take action in their own lives. Their actions resulted in million-dollar companies, breakthrough ideas known all around the world, and international recognition.

This book is for anyone who wants to change their life for the better, create more opportunities, or who is seeking something new. You can gain new inspiration and ideas from the uplifting examples of people I have exclusively spoken with and gained valuable information from such as:

- The world's leading expert on how to license a product idea and his journey of becoming an inspiration to millions.
- An artist who became the cofounder of a billion-dollar company because of a need to solve his own problem.
- The creator of the cell phone.
- An entrepreneur whose one-of-a-kind approach to creating a game has sold 32,000,000 games worldwide.
- The longest-serving CEO in Silicon Valley.

All of these individuals have taken different paths to get to where they are, yet they have a common element that persists in their lives. They take massive action. Knowing how and when to take such action is equally important. As you read the inspiring examples within this book, make note of the golden nuggets you can start to emulate in your own life.

PART 1

THE POWER OF THE START

CHAPTER 1

START NOW

IF NOT NOW, WHEN?

"The secret to getting ahead is getting started."

—MARK TWAIN

Starting something new can be tough. This is why many delay the process. I have learned it is much better to start now and learn than to delay something and get distracted. Many years ago, I had made sure to replace television watching with goal achievement. I still keep this practice. When I tell people that I don't watch television, they are usually surprised. I think this is a very productive habit, and it is beneficial to navigate attention to more progressive uses. I am now a five-time coauthor with many of them on a best sellers list. I can contribute this to making good use of my time and this is one of the main reasons why I was able to start at a relatively young age. Another reward is that I have been featured in top publications such as the *Huffington Post*, *CNN*, as well as over a dozen more.

The key to finding success is to Start Now.

NOW OR NEVER

"If you do something where you are uncomfortable, you will become familiar with what it is like being uncomfortable."

—JIM MCKELVEY

Starting now can be uncomfortable. However, we have to continue to overcome these feelings until we are able to conquer these same exact feelings. An example of this is Jim McKelvey. Jim McKelvey is a true innovator at heart. When I interviewed him, I learned he is someone who is not scared to start the newest and most unpredictable initiatives.

He is also an artist, self-proclaimed nerd, author, and serial entrepreneur. He is fueled by the opportunity to create new and improved products and services. As a university student in his freshman year, Jim took a School of Engineering computer class that had used a textbook the professor had actually written (Meyerowitz, 2011). Since Jim did not like this textbook, he had written his own textbook and sold it to a publisher on a dare. A very ambitious thing to do. The textbook had been seen as an advanced demonstration of the problem-solving mentality his school encouraged (Carriere, 2018). Starting this led to Jim's streak of successful innovation, but it was not without pain.

In 1989, in St. Louis Missouri, when Jim was around twenty-four years old working as a glassblower, his mother died. He then started to reevaluate his life and decided one of the things he had not done in his life was something great (Meyerowitz, 2011). After this realization, he had decided to start a computer company called Mira. He was able to grow this company substantially—that is, until the Internet had nearly taken the company out. However, as an innovator, Jim had made Mira into a digital publishing company which is still in operation.

Mira was also where Jim had met fifteen-year-old Jack Dorsey who is now both the CEO of Square and Twitter. Back then, he was still in high school and had even pulled an all-nighter as an intern for Jim on his first day. Little did Jim know that in the future this intern would grow up to be his boss.

Jim had decided to leave Mira in the hands of his managers because it got to the point it could exist without him. He then went on to work on a hobby he loved, which was glassblowing, not knowing what was to come. One day at his art studio, a woman from Panama had called him and showed interest in buying one of his glass pieces for $2,000, which was a big deal at the time (McKelvey, n.d.). However, the purchase could not be made because she had an American Express card and Jim did not accept those then; he had only accepted Visa and MasterCard. After this lost sale, Jim had vented about it to Jack. He had told him how the iPhone has everything needed to have saved the sale. He then came up with the idea to build a payment system to prevent little businesses from getting overcharged (Meyerowitz, 2011).

Now, Jim along with Twitter's cofounder Jack Dorsey set out to create the groundbreaking company called Square. The product was innovative, and nothing else was like it on the market. However, the real reason they created the company was to get even with Twitter. Jack had been let go from the new company he had cofounded, and now he and Jim were going to create a brand-new company. They had been looking for a good business idea and now they had finally found it.

Having already worked together before, they started creating a new company together. When designing the product for Square, Jim, as an artist, had two designs to choose from for their Square reader: one with a long track design and one with a short track design. The long track design read credit cards perfectly and according to Jim did not look cool, but the short track worked.

Jim decided to release the short track version of their Square reader because people seemed to enjoy this version more as well. Jim said, "When I tested the short one, they were just blown away. And so even though the short one was more difficult to use, I released it as the product because it got people's attention. And the fact that it was slightly difficult to use, I think, was ultimately good for us, because it gave people a reason to focus on not just the reader, which was difficult to use, but also all the other stuff Square was about. So, while they were playing with our reader, they were also thinking about how we didn't lock them into a contract, how our prices are really fair, how we would settle their money three days faster than anybody else. All this other stuff we were doing became the thing worth focusing on. So instead of spending two seconds thinking about my product, they were spending two minutes thinking about my product, and that's a huge difference."

With persuasion and persistence, they were able to convince executives in the industry to accept their product. After Square had finally gained the approval of the financial industry to operate, they started to grow at a monumental rate. Within a few years, they had reached billion-dollar status. However, this was when the real issue began.

After seeing such growth, a major competitor showed up. This competitor has been known to beat every company it decided to go after and copy. This company was Amazon. In 2014, when Square was just a four-year-old company, Amazon copied their product. In an interview I had with Jim in 2020, he said, "Amazon typically wins when they do the following thing; they copy your product, they undercut your price by 30 percent, and then they add the Amazon brand, and they've always won using that formula. Except in Square's case, they didn't win."

This frightening competition with Amazon had lasted over a year, and it was a very stressful time for Square. But they kept going. The Innovation Stack is what Jim credits for finally being able to win the competition with Amazon. He said, "If you are doing something new and different enough in the marketplace, copying it becomes super difficult, even for companies like Amazon." After a year of launching their card reader, Amazon had surprisingly stopped making them and had also mailed a Square reader to all of their existing customers. They had apparently learned that the complexity of Square's Innovation Stack was more than they had anticipated, so they backed out of the competition with Square. This was a monumental win for Jim.

Jim's company Square has given merchants and small businesses the ability to accept credit card payments using their smartphones. Before Square's invention, merchants and small businesses had few options to accept credit card payments without costly merchant service fees, which meant many merchants and small businesses had to opt out of accepting credit cards altogether.

Jim McKelvey had no experience in the banking industry before he had created Square, but he didn't let that stop him on his quest to help merchants and small businesses succeed without being overcharged. Being a continual supporter of the underdog, he states, "If you trace back the history of some of our greatest inventions, the people at the founding moment were not qualified to do what they did. The Wright brothers—they were not qualified to be the first people in the air. IKEA was founded by a seventeen-year-old kid. It's the biggest furniture company in the world right now. What does a seventeen-year-old kid know? The biggest bank in the world was started by a kid who dropped out of school at age fifteen and became a produce vendor. Think about the world of banking being totally upended by a guy who sold lettuce. These are fantastic stories" (Fenske, 2020).

Jim's boldness has not only helped create an innovative and helpful solution for many merchants and small businesses as well as larger corporations such as Whole Foods, but it has also helped inspire many budding entrepreneurs and inventors around the world. He had taken on the financial industry as a start-up, overcoming the rules and regulations surrounding the industry and today, his company Square continues to thrive and has even added several new innovative services such as Cash App, which allows users to transfer money to one another using just a mobile phone app. Jim McKelvey is a great example of perseverance, and he shows us that anyone can accomplish their goals if they are willing to take the action required to do so.

THE TIME IS NOW
In a group meeting with Guy Kawasaki, who was a Chief Evangelist at Apple, I had asked him about how he prepares to take action on things he is interested in doing. I wanted to know how a go-getter like himself goes about accomplishing a wide variety of achievements. His response to me was, "I just start. When I decided to do a podcast, I just jumped in, I didn't do background research; I just decided to do it. And that's been the story of my life. At forty-four, I decided to play hockey. At sixty, I decided to take up surfing[…]I believe in a growth mindset. When you fall in love with something, you're not going to be asking yourself and over intellectualizing; you're just going to frickin' do it!" This struck me. His response is how we all should go about doing new things since it starts with a positive mindset.

What an example and reminder that age doesn't have to define us. We can do anything we want when we decide to start.

Each one of us has to start somewhere and age should not be a factor in our decision. Often, we may stop ourselves from doing things we may enjoy because we may feel we are past the age of doing so or are too young, but it is more important that we give ourselves the chance to succeed.

RISK AND LEARN

"Take risks now and do something bold. You won't regret it."

—ELON MUSK

Massive action is the number one habit of Tesla's founder, Elon Musk. As someone constantly on the move, he is creating innovations that only seemed possible in dreams through his continuous and relentless action. Along with Tesla, Elon Musk is the founder of multiple companies including SpaceX, an aerospace manufacturer and space transportation services company that has the tremendous goal of enabling the colonization of Mars (SpaceX, n.d.).

Elon Musk was born in South Africa. As a child, he was different. He gravitated toward books and daydreams. His daydreams would worry his parents because of their frequency. Luckily, he was a bright child that was daydreaming about new inventions. His mother stated, "He goes into his brain and then you just see he is in another world. He still does that. Now I just leave him be because I know he is designing a new rocket or something" (Mejia, 2018). At the age of twelve, he had the ability to program computers and sold his first software, which was a game for $500 (Gravier, 2020). This is the age when much of his early entrepreneurial streak had begun. As smart and capable as he was, he has stated that he had a terrible upbringing and a lot of adversity growing up. He was bullied until the age of fifteen and was finally able to defend himself through a growth spurt and by learning karate, judo, and wrestling; he was not going to be pushed down a flight of stairs ever again.

At the age of twenty-seven, he had sold his very first tech company, Zip2, for $307 million in 1999, receiving twenty-two million dollars for the 7 percent share he owned (Mann, 2021). Instead of spending it all on frivolous things like many twenty-something-year-olds, he invested some of his earnings into another company, which is still going strong today, called PayPal. However, at the time, it was named X.com. After the acquisition of PayPal, Elon stated, "Going from PayPal, I thought, 'Well, what are some of the other problems that are likely to most affect the future of humanity?'"

He then went on to start Tesla. See the pattern?

Elon continues his pursuit to innovate not for the profits but for his love of creating new and exciting things. His relentless drive has resulted in acquiring present leadership roles at SpaceX, Tesla, The Boring Company, SolarCity, Hyperloop, and Neuralink; all of which are innovating new technologies and industries. He is on a level that takes a lot of skill and knowledge. He has pursued learning vigorously. As well as learned how to learn. He states, "One bit of advice: It is important to view knowledge as sort of a semantic tree—make sure you understand the fundamental principles, i.e., the trunk and big branches, before you get into the leaves/details or there is nothing for them to hang on to."

He is in the pursuit to bring dreams to life. Managing his hectic schedule, which often includes a day packed with work and work-related activities, he is someone who is definitely on the move and stays ahead of the competition. In the past, when competition pushed him into a corner; he managed to bounce back by continuing to push forward. With this type of action-oriented mentality; anything is possible. This strategy has helped propel him to where he is today.

Being the founder of several successful companies is not an easy feat. However, with the right knowledge and skills and taking massive action; it can be done. In his mission to grow his companies, he has made it a point to be a present CEO often working alongside his employees on the factory floor (Clifford, 2018). When he had to pause his company, Tesla, during the pandemic, he quickly moved to another state in the US to be able to continue being able to build and grow his companies (Somerville, 2020). Relentless and constant action is a key to his success.

When working, he multitasks and will often have lunch during meetings. Most of his working hours are accounted for, and this has been important to be able to keep up with the demands of his companies. He has shared, "Persistence is very important. You should not give up unless you are forced to give up" (Economy, 2016). This attitude is exactly what has helped his companies to become successful. He doesn't give up and makes sure he does what is needed to succeed.

"The path to success is to take massive, determined action." This quote by Tony Robbins sums up Elon's work ethic adequately. Elon has been taking massive action since his youth and hasn't stopped yet. In January of 2021, Elon had reportedly become the wealthiest man in the world. His response to this report was, "Well, back to work…"

OPPORTUNITIES

"Do what you can, with what you have, where you are."
— THEODORE ROOSEVELT

When opportunity arose, people like Levi Strauss, the founder of the first company to manufacture blue jeans, had traveled to San Francisco, California, to seek a fortune during the famed California Gold Rush of 1849. However, he wasn't like most of the travelers there. He thought differently. Instead of trying to strike it rich through finding gold in the rivers, he sold the influx of people clothing, fabric, bedding, and tools among other things. The most prosperous were the blue jeans he had invented. These blue jeans were made to be a more durable piece of clothing that miners could wear. This led to him becoming more successful than most of the miners. He found a way to expand his business at the right time. If he would have waited, then there may not have been this opportunity available to him, and we would not have our beloved blue jeans.

LEARNING THROUGH ACTION

When given an opportunity that you know will lead to a positive outcome, it is best to act now and start. There is no need to wait. This is a way to gain experience and knowledge. Jim McKelvey and Elon Musk both had started their world-changing companies without having any experience in the industries they had conquered. Since they decided to take the initiative and start creating their concepts, they had found a way to make them real. If we all decided to start now, then we would all have less regrets in the future.

> "This generation has a responsibility to reshape the world. Start the task even if it will not be fulfilled in your lifetime. Even if it seems hopeless now, never give up. Offer a positive vision, with enthusiasm and joy, and an optimistic outlook."
>
> —DALAI LAMA

START NOW ASSESSMENT

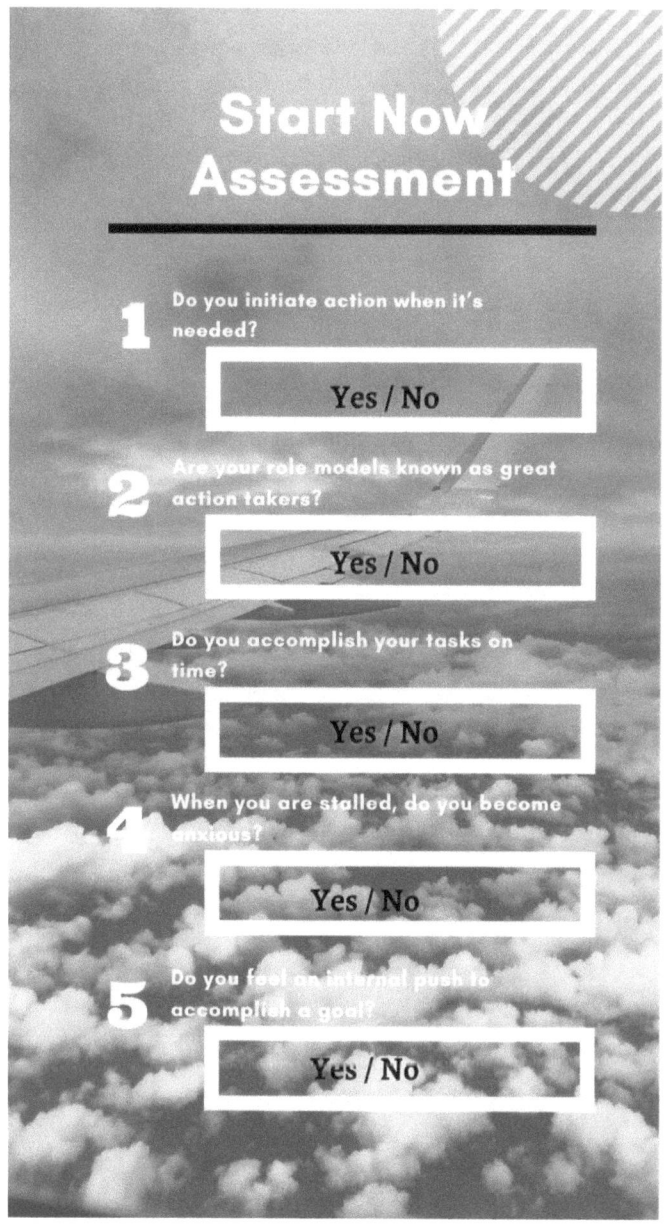

Start Now Assessment

1. Do you initiate action when it's needed?

   Yes / No

2. Are your role models known as great action takers?

   Yes / No

3. Do you accomplish your tasks on time?

   Yes / No

4. When you are stalled, do you become anxious?

   Yes / No

5. Do you feel an internal push to accomplish a goal?

   Yes / No

Answers:
Add up the number of times you chose "Yes."
5/5 - Awesome! You are an action dynamo and tend to start things fast.
4/5 - Good! You are an action-oriented person.
3/5 - Almost ready! You want to become more action-oriented and can get there if you try.
2/5 - Needs improvement, but you can do better with practice.
1/5 - Alert. Try implementing strategies from this book and see your score rise!

CHAPTER 2

THE POWER OF MOMENTUM

"The most important thing you can do to achieve your goals is to make sure that as soon as you set them you immediately begin to create momentum."

—TONY ROBBINS

The pressure was building. This was it; we had to come up with our second business idea…on the second-to-last day of the competition. The competing teams were not having this issue. As I grew frustrated with a teammate for nit-picking at our original idea, we realized another company had already come out with our idea; though they were small, it was enough to make us want to change our game plan. "Let's go for a walk," suggested one of my teammates. We then got away from the competing teams and had a walking meeting. The fresh air and warm sunny day made it easier to think.

We each came up with an idea to work on and decided on the final one together. It sounded good. Then, we started coming up with the features it would have. It was getting better.

Wow, for a fifteen-minute or so walk, we were on a roll.

You see, we had to do something different to get us to a new place to have the ability to build new momentum. It wasn't extreme, but it worked.

The Power of Momentum is not normally taught in school. However, it is extremely important.

Newton's first law of motion states that an object at rest stays at rest, and an object in motion stays in motion with the same speed and in the same direction unless acted upon by an unbalanced force. This exact principle can be applied to our lives daily. This principle can also be described as momentum. Our actions compound and generate opportunity for us. Choosing the best actions to take can require trial and error. These trial and errors can be done in a way that creates innovation. There have been many times when what had seemed like a mistake was, in fact, a solution to a problem.

This is what Joseph McVicker did. In the early 1950s, Joseph McVicker created the famous Play-Doh that children play with today. However, he had originally created it to remove the soot in coal-burning homes. Soon after he created this idea, people started to switch from coal to gas to heat their homes. There was no longer an important need for his product. The company he was working in was heading toward bankruptcy. What was he to do? Luckily, soon after, he had heard his sister—who was a teacher—was using the dough he made as modeling clay for her classes. She persuaded him to start manufacturing the product as a children's toy. Joseph McVicker took her advice; Play-Doh became a hit and is still being sold until this day. Over two billion units have been sold. This invention may not have been as successful if it had been used for its original purpose.

If Joseph had not created the dough in the first place, he would not have had the chance for it to create the momentum it did. However, since he had created it, even though it was in the wrong timing, he was able to evolve it into something different that many children play with even now. You may even have played with it yourself!

How many times have you had an idea but did not implement it? If you are like most of us, plenty of times! I have heard of many ideas from people who have had a unique solution to a problem, yet did not take action. They wait for someone else to come up with the solution. I think it is important to take the steps to actually try; this is where the momentum begins.

Coincidentally, I started my journalism career this way. One of my very first interviews was with a public figure whom I had looked up to for a very long time. He not only had an impressive career but was surrounded by people who did as well. I took that opportunity and said yes. Not only did I learn a lot from this opportunity, but it gave me more confidence to keep pursuing the things I wanted to do. It was the starting point of my journalism career.

KEEP IT GOING

"I think if you do something and it turns out pretty good, then you should go do something else wonderful, not dwell on it for too long. Just figure out what's next."

—STEVE JOBS

Steve Jobs was a great example of an action taker. He knew how to build momentum. He was the cofounder and CEO of Apple Inc. and also the CEO of Pixar, a computer animation studio known for creating feature films including *Toy Story*, which was the third highest grossing animated film of all time upon its release. Although he achieved great success in his career, he didn't always have a successful life, especially as a child. His story began on February 24, 1955, in San Francisco, California, where he was born and adopted by a married couple. His adoption was not easy. His birth mother had refused to sign his final adoption papers and had taken his adoptive parents to court. She agreed a few months later to the adoption only when his parents had made a promise he would go to college.

His school years were difficult for him as he was hard to discipline and had been bullied. However, he was able to relocate to a new middle school, which helped mitigate the issue. In high school, he found a passion for electronics as well as literature, yet in college, he dropped out without telling his parents. This was a big deal as his adoptive parents had promised his birth mother that he would go to college. Instead, he started working at Atari and became a technician, and months later after he started, he went on a trip to India. Steve took this seven-month trip to India to search for enlightenment, but he did not find the enlightenment he sought. He did, however, embrace meditation for the rest of his life.

Two years later, his friend, Steve Wozniak had created a basic design of the Apple I computer, which Steve Jobs then had the idea to sell. They had both financed its creation by selling their personal belongings. Steve Jobs had realized there was an opportunity in the computer market because, at the time, computers were very large and could almost fill an entire room. They were also very costly, and most people did not own one. Together, Steve Jobs and Steve Wozniak took the Apple I, which was a desktop computer that came as a single motherboard and was preassembled, and created a company we now know today as Apple. One year later, they also created Apple II, their second product. Steve Jobs had now opened an entirely new market, the personal computer (Ho-Jo, n.d.).

In 1984, they introduced their most successful product yet: the Macintosh computer. Steve Jobs was committed to growing his company with new and innovative products. He was excelling as a leader and made sure he hired smart people. He had started to become a leader who was open to doing things differently. It worked. His strategies included hiring passionate problem solvers instead of those with polished resumes. Also, he believed that instead of directing employees on how to do their job, that leadership should be focused on articulating that shared vision so everyone could be working toward the same goal (Mikel, 2017). He had changed the way things were done in the corporate world and was a force to be reckoned with.

Apple was growing rapidly, but even with all its success, Steve Jobs was forced from the company in 1985, only one year after releasing his most successful product. He was let go from the company after a heated disagreement. That same year, he started NeXT, Inc., which was his second computer company. He was quick to move on and create a new endeavor. During this time, he also acquired Pixar Animation Studios. He didn't become as successful from NeXT, Inc. as he may have hoped; he did, however, become successful with his company Pixar. When Pixar went public, he became a billionaire.

Steve Job's new wealth had mostly come from Pixar and only a fraction had come from Apple. He was seeing greater success with Pixar than he had with Apple, yet he decided to go back to Apple as its CEO in 1997. He was brought back to save the company he had started, which was being overtaken by competitors. He had now also become a better leader yet again and had to make harder decisions. One of which was letting go of about three thousand employees. He had realized Apple was creating too many of the same versions of products and decided to reduce them. He reduced Apple's products by a surprising 70 percent. He stated, "Deciding what not to do is as important as deciding what to do."

His new strategy for Apple was to have only four products, including only one desktop and one portable device for both consumers and professionals. He simplified the company. This move helped the company to finally regain its profits. Within two years, Steve Jobs was able to save the company. When the company was doing well again, he focused on innovation: the iPod portable digital audio player, the Apple iTunes Store, the iPhone, and the iPad tablet computer. Many of the products are still used today.

As the founder of the company, Steve Jobs knew about the company more than most others may have at the time, including its executives. He was able to make quick and impactful decisions that may have been too difficult for another to make in his position. The decision for Steve Jobs to go back to Apple was a good one, as he not only had a vision for Apple, but he also cared for the company. He believed that work fills a large part of our life, and the only way to be truly satisfied is to do work we believe is great.

> *"The only way to do great work is to love what you do. If you haven't found it yet, keep looking. Don't settle. As with all matters of the heart, you'll know when you find it. And, like any great relationship, it just gets better and better as the years roll on. So, keep looking until you find it. Don't settle."*
>
> —STEVE JOBS

He seemed to know that when you are doing something you love, it is easier to build the momentum you need.

His decision to go back to Apple was made thoughtfully. Steve Jobs did not need to go back; they needed him. He was already successful. He had a vision for his company, and this vision was "to make a contribution to the world by making tools for the mind that advance humankind" (Investopedia, 2021). His vision for Apple had meaning. When he would explain this vision to others, they would become almost mesmerized by his charisma (Gallo, 2019). He also had an intensity that helped others listen to what he had to say. These were valuable traits to him and helped him take his company to great heights. He was a great marketer.

Since Steve Jobs cared deeply for his company, his expectations were high. He showed passion and wholeheartedly believed in perfecting his products. At times, this made him difficult to work with. He was called "rude, dismissive, hostile, spiteful" (Greenfield, 2013) by some of those he worked with. However, as he got older, these traits had minimized greatly. He had become kinder and fairer to other people (Musil, 2012). He often started to speak about inspirational topics aside from his companies. He had realized at the end of his life that there was a greater meaning than success, commenting, "Almost everything, all external expectations, all pride, all fear of embarrassment or failure, these things just fall away in the face of death, leaving only what is truly important."

Steve Jobs was ahead of his time. He was a pioneer and visionary constantly building new solutions. He had big dreams and goals and also was not afraid to go after them. He achieved this through momentum. This very momentum helped him build products that have changed the world as well as make his company one of the greatest technology companies of all time, which has touched over a billion lives.

Recently, Apple has become the world's first publicly traded company to reach a one-trillion-dollar valuation.

Steve Jobs by happenstance was a big motivator for me to get into the business world at an early age. I had always wanted to have my own businesses growing up. After reading his biography by Walter Isaacson, I made the moves to do so. It was such an eye-opening experience as every business has different factors that play a role in its success. You just have to find those factors. I learned that getting mentors and seeking advice and strategies to grow your business is one of the most important things you can do. I learned it is in the momentum that brings a business's success, not in getting it right the first time. There is no perfection—only progress as the business world is always changing.

An acquaintance of mine, Alec Stern, the cofounder of Constant Contact, also uses this momentum principle in his life. Having had the honor to speak with him on several occasions, I learned that whenever he has positive momentum in his life, he continues to build upon it. His strategy involves his lucky song, "Don't Stop Believin'" in order to get himself into a positive mindset so he can build the momentum he needs. Then, he gets to working so he can put that positive momentum into use.

POWER OF NOT GIVING IN
"Procrastination is the enemy of success and the guilt of not doing something always steals your energy."
—BARBARA CORCORAN

Barbara Corcoran is a businesswoman, investor, and current Shark on the multi-Emmy-Award-winning show, *Shark Tank*. Although she had started a five-billion-dollar company called The Corcoran Group, it wasn't all smooth sailing. She had actually started her company with a $1,000 loan and no prior experience in running a business.

She had twenty jobs by the time she turned twenty-three (Elkins, 2018). This is more than most people have had in their whole lifetime. She didn't quite seem to fit into any of the jobs she had tried to pursue. Although she had a degree in education and had been a schoolteacher for about one year, she continued to look for other opportunities, including renting out New York City apartments, selling hot dogs, dispatching newspapers, selling books, and several other pursuits.

In 1973 while working in New Jersey, she had borrowed $1,000 from a friend and had started a real estate company in New York. Within two years, the company had fourteen agents and a half million dollars in sales (Jacobson, 2018). She was still in her twenties. With her dreams coming true at a high speed, things took an unexpected turn years later when a real estate market crash hit her company hard.

Many of the real estate companies had started to go out of business, and Barbara's almost did as well. She started to write her goodbye speech when suddenly, she remembered a vivid childhood memory. That memory was of her mom taking her and her siblings to a children's farm. At the farm, they would watch fancy New Yorkers lining up and buying Jack Russell puppies. She had noticed the New

Yorkers had tension and were arguing and had recognized it was because the farmer's wife had invited everyone at the same time to buy a puppy and there were not enough puppies for everyone. Only around half of the people in line would get one.

She used this memory as the solution to her problem. She was going to use this lesson to now sell eighty-eight properties owned by a big insurance company that had not been sold yet. She took all the properties, averaged out the prices, and priced them exactly the same, and quietly told her salespeople at their next meeting about the "secret sale" instead of her previous announcement of going out of business. This worked and all eighty-eight properties were sold in a short period. "We had over a hundred and fifty people hours before the sales standing in line in the worst real estate market the city had ever seen on the heels of the stock market crashing." She learned that it is all in how you position it. She knew that if she could create buzz around the properties, then it would build the momentum needed to bring in buyers.

Soon after her business started to thrive again, her personal life had taken a turn and Barbara had to heal for a year, but she came back swinging. Even after being demeaned by a former ex, Barbara thrived. In 2001, she was able to have more sales in real estate than any of her competitors in New York City. "What drove me was simply my determination not to have anybody laugh at me ever again." She had become a "queen" of New York real estate. She thinks that what is important is to figure out that one move you could continue to use again in your "drawer of blades."

"The gimmick that I used building my company from the first year to the twenty-fifth year when I sold it for an outrageous amount of money was creating a market report that is open to anybody in any business. Give them statistics on your own business to reporters, as many as you can. I got so much press coverage. I honestly stole the market share by stealing the limelight because I was constantly in the press reporting on statistics…and that frankly is the big kahuna of building businesses that so few companies take advantage of."

Barbara used the power of momentum well in growing her business in such a crowded market, and she did so openly.

Giving honest advice is what Barbara Corcoran is known for. She is open to sharing what has worked for her as well as what did not in her career, which is not what most people are willing to do. This is why she is one of the favorite judges on the hit business show, *Shark Tank*. Barbara has appeared on the show for all twelve seasons. She had even signed the original contract for it without even reading it. She knew it was being produced by one of the biggest television producers at the time, Mark Burnett, who had already produced shows such as *Survivor*. After she sent back the signed contract, she started to prepare because she thought she was going to Hollywood.

Only four days before she was going to fly to LA for the show, she got a phone call. She was told there was a change of mind and someone else was going to take her place. Instead of accepting the change, Barbara immediately took action. She started to write him an email with the intention of getting back her offer. The letter started with, "I understand you've asked another girl to dance instead of me. Although I appreciate being reserved as a fallback, I'm much more accustomed to coming in first." She then gave several examples of the many times she had succeeded amid difficulties.

Another detail in her letter was a proposition. The proposition was to invite both of them. She wrote, "If you have both ladies in LA, you can mix it up a bit and see which personalities make the best combination for your show. I've found in building teams myself that the combination of personalities is always more important than the expertise or strengths of single individuals. You may even drop a man for me because, believe it or not, I'm just as smart and mean as the next guy."

Lastly, in the third paragraph she wrote, she talked about how she would be great for the role, and she was able to market herself efficiently. She was given the role, but this time, it was solid. She has been on the show now for over a decade, and she credits the opportunity to this letter. If Barbara hadn't taken the initiative to get back what was originally given to her, we may not have known about Barbara today. Her resilience is what has brought her much of the success she has now.

After consistent setbacks throughout her life, Barabara Corcoran has established herself as a go-to businesswoman.

She has not let much deter her from reaching her goals. In both the real estate market and the entertainment industry, Barbara Corcoran has taken action in the face of near setbacks and has emerged victorious. She forged ahead with her ideas and built tremendous momentum as she went and continues to do.

"You don't have to get it right, you just have to get it going."
—BARBARA CORCORAN

The Power of Momentum is very underutilized today. We become so distracted in our day-to-day life that we forget if we take just small amounts of time each day or even each week to work on what we want to accomplish, we can actually make progress. So, challenge yourself to take out a calendar and block out an amount of time each day to work on something that is important to you.

MOMENTUM ASSESSMENT

Momentum Assessment

1 When you start to make progress, do you make plans for a newer goal?

Yes / No

2 When seeing someone doing better than you, do you move onto something else?

Yes / No

3 Have you delayed a goal to wait for better timing?

Yes / No

4 Do you not take opportunities because you think they'll come again?

Yes / No

5 Do you dream more than do?

Yes / No

Answers:
Add up the number of times you chose "No."
5/5 - You are a momentum expert! You know how to get things going.
4/5 - Good! You know how to build momentum when needed.
3/5 - Close! Making the right choices will drastically increase your momentum creating ability.
2/5 - Can use adjustment. With the right strategies, you can create more momentum.
1/5 - You're in luck! You can try again, but this time make sure to follow the momentum building strategies in this book first.

CHAPTER 3

WHY START AT THIS MOMENT?

THE ULTIMATE REWARD

What is your Ultimate Reward? Have you ever asked yourself that? I am sure you have, but in another way. When I was young, it was a tiny island with one palm tree (two if I was feeling ambitious) and a little sailing boat on the side. The sun always shined. A little unrealistic, right?

Yes, now as I've grown older, I can see how unrealistic that dream really was. Now I wonder, "Why so small?" I can put a resort on that island. I can put a house on that island or anything else I want since it is my dream and, ultimately, my Ultimate Reward. Ultimate Rewards change, but at the root, it is your decision on what they will be.

"Your time is limited, so don't waste it living someone else's life."
—STEVE JOBS

Martin Cooper is the father of the cell phone. His invention gave us the ability to be able to communicate with each other all over the world. How many of us can say they have met the inventor of the cell phone? It is one of my favorite experiences, and I will always remember his thoughtful compliment to me: "You're among the nicer people I've talked to" (regarding journalists). I was also inspired from our conversation of his motivation to continue to create helpful technology. I was able to learn a lot from him. Having always been curious, this trait has helped him tremendously over the years.

Martin was born on December 26, 1928, in Chicago, Illinois. He had known he was going to be into something technical when he grew up, so he had gone to a technical high school. An early experience had helped him spark this curiosity that he still remembers to this day. It was when he was about five years old; he was fascinated with how some boys were able to burn paper by using a magnifying glass. He then went on to receive a Master of Science in Electrical Engineering from the Illinois Institute of Technology.

This degree served him well as he started to eventually work for Motorola, Inc. as the senior development engineer in the mobile equipment group. The transforming moment for Martin came after he had heard about what Bell Systems was thinking about doing. At the time, they were the biggest company in the world. They wanted to release cellular technology to help connect people better, but they were going to use it in cars. This did not make sense to Martin. "So just imagine that, that we had been trapped in our homes, tied to our desks by this telephone wire, and now the Bell Systems was going to trap us in our cars, and that didn't make any sense to us."

Martin had greater plans for cellular technology. However, it was a big risk. Bell Systems was one of the most powerful companies at the time and taking them on was going to be difficult. He knew he needed to do something right away. He went to the FCC and told them it was wrong and they should not allow Bell Systems to keep us stuck in our cars. He felt so strongly about the issue that he continued the battle for thirteen years. "We believed people didn't want to talk in cars and that people wanted to talk to other people" (Loeffler, 2021).

Meanwhile, he had gotten the support of his bosses, chairman of his company, as well as the president of his company, to start putting a team together of great engineers and designers. This team built the first cell phone, which required them to build entirely different parts that did not exist at the time yet.

In only three months, starting in December and ending in March, they had a working cell phone. This was huge. It weighed over two pounds and had a battery life of twenty-five minutes, but it was a sign of things to come.

It was now time to show the world their creation.

The night before they did the first demonstration, Martin and his team were in the Hilton Hotel in New York, in the suite Richard Burton and Elizabeth Taylor were known to stay in when they were in New York. They were still working on the phone and fixing problems the night before their live demonstration. They even had a spare phone in case their main one didn't work.

On April 3, 1973, Martin made the first public cell phone call. He reached into his pocket, took out his paper address book, and he looked up the number of his main competitor and dialed it. He wanted to give him the big news.

During the phone call, Martin said, "I'm calling you from a cell phone, with a *real* cell phone. A handheld personal portable cell phone." There was silence on the other line. This demonstration had helped Martin and his company gain Federal Communications Commission (FCC) approval for cellular licenses to be assigned to competing entities and prevented an AT&T monopoly on cellular service (Marty, 2020).

It took a decade after the demonstration for the cell phone to get to market. Once released to the public, it had a cost of $3,500, which is about $7,000 today. He envisioned in the future that cell phone technology would be so small it could be hung on an ear or even embedded under the skin.

Martin invented the cell phone over forty-eight years ago. If he had not taken the initiative to start when it was needed, there would have been a monopoly on the technology, which might have made it difficult for anyone to have had cell phones in the future. His invention has made our lives easier and more connected. "Even though I conceived of it, it really took teamwork, and literally hundreds of people ended up creating the vision of what cellular is today, which by the way is not complete. We are still working on it and still trying to make it better" (Shiels, 2003).

"Don't do anything unless you're passionate about it because there are no easy businesses. This is rule number one."
—MARTIN COOPER

ABUNDANCE

There was a man who loved homemade apple cider, but it was hard to come by in his small town during most of the year. He decided to grow his own apple trees and make his own cider so he could have his own supply. "How wonderful! I can have fresh cider whenever I want," he said. Since he had a good amount of land, he started to plan his next steps. He went to visit some of the local farmers to ask them about what he needed to go about his plan. He learned, to his dismay, that apple trees can take three to five years to produce fruit. He decided to let his plan go; he did not want to wait that long to grow apples.

Three years went by, and the man was visiting with an old friend who offered him a drink. "This is great! Where did you get this?" the man asked, thinking his friend had bought it. The friend then replied, "From my trees! When we talked about your idea about planting your own apple trees, it inspired me to do the same. I have a lot of land, so I thought, why not?"

To the man's surprise, his friend had immediately planted the apple trees after their first conversation and was now reaping their fruits. Not only was his friend enjoying having his own abundance, but he had enough to sell to the local stores and restaurants.

Starting now is so important. It plants the seeds for the future. When we start at this moment, we begin to take off.

So, how can people start at this moment and make the traction that they want? First, make sure you choose the right goals. Many top leaders have a "do not do" list. Yes, they actually have a do not do list because if they say yes too often to everything, it will distract them from the important tasks they need their time and energy for. When people progress, they find out that if they allow it, they will become overcome with unnecessary distractions that will burn them out sooner rather than later. We don't want that. So, when we start to take action in our lives, we need to make sure what we are saying yes to things that align us with our final goals.

There have been moments where my time has been needed in several different places at once. If I would have agreed to those requests, they would have hindered the quality of my other work. Not only that, but it would also have exhausted me as well. As much as we want to do everything, it is key to make sure we prioritize our work and stick to it without getting distracted. We have to prioritize the quality of our work before quantity. An example of this is Apple.

If Apple prioritized quantity over quality, would they even be as successful as they are today? I do not think so. In a group meeting I had with Steve Wozniak, the cofounder of Apple, he talked about his passion for technology, how he would have spent all his money on a computer before a house. Now that is passion. When you have this kind of passion for what you do, it won't be hard to start now.

Everyone has started somewhere, and it wasn't always easy. This is okay. It is completely okay if things are hard; this does not by any means imply that things will always be hard or that you cannot do it. If everyone gave up the first time things got hard, would we have the mind-blowing inventions we have today?

Most people who have started many of the inventions we are so privileged to have now came from people who have been told it wasn't possible, they are crazy, and they should move on. I think if someone is naive to think something can't be done by now when we have so many innovations in our everyday life as proof that the seemingly impossible is indeed in fact possible, then they are the ones who need to move on.

PROGRESSION OBSESSION

"Be impatient. It will create the progress the world needs."
—SUNDAR PICHAI

Sundar Pichai is the CEO of Google and Alphabet, Inc. He was born on June 10, 1972, in India. As a child, he was interested in technology. He was also talented at remembering numbers. His family had realized that he could recall every phone number that he had ever dialed on their phone (Who Is, 2019). His family worked hard to give him a good education and it paid off. He created his first digital game when he was still in school, which was a chess game.

He did so well in school that he was given a scholarship to Stanford University. This was monumental for him as it would shape his life forever; as well as the entire world's. Since he had dreams of Silicon Valley, he had made sure to accept this opportunity even though he would only arrive in California with a couple hundred dollars from his family. He would have to figure something out when he arrived. "My father spent the equivalent of a year's salary on my plane ticket to the US so I could attend Stanford. It was my first time ever on a plane" (Pichai, 2014).

Sundar did well when he arrived in California. He had graduated with a master's from Stanford University and then went on to get an MBA from the University of Pennsylvania's Wharton School. Then the trajectory of his life was formed when he interviewed at Google on April Fool's Day in 2004, which coincidentally was the same day the company had launched Gmail.

Knowing that Gmail has been the world's most popular email provider for almost a decade now, this was great timing for Sundar to start working at Google. At the time, however, Sundar thought that the free email service was a prank that the company was making.

One of the first projects that Sundar started working on at Google was the search toolbar feature. Two years later, in 2006, Microsoft had their own search engine called Bing as the new default search engine on Internet Explorer. Amazingly, Sundar was able to help convince computer manufacturers to preinstall the Google Toolbar on their hardware

(Who Is, 2019). This helped Google to stay relevant. Sundar was so focused on Google's success that he had even convinced Google's cofounders Larry Page and Sergey Brin to build their own company browser.

This had turned out to become what is now known as Google Chrome, the world's most valued search engine, which has led to Google becoming one of the world's top leading companies.

He didn't stop there. After this successful idea, he started to work on their Android One project, which was Google's initiative to make low-cost smartphones for "the next five billion" people coming online (Who Is, 2019). During Sundar's time and increasing success at Google, he received interest from competing companies such as Twitter. To keep Sundar, Google offered him a substantial package to continue working there. This was a great call. Sundar had a hand in growing Chrome OS, Google Drive, and had overseen Gmail and Google Maps. All of which are doing well today.

Knowing early on that he had an interest in technology, Sundar made sure to start embracing this early on. By doing so, he continued to make moves throughout his life directing him in the right direction, which has led to his early success. His experience had given him the confidence he needed to excel in his career, even in the early years. Now, he has become the CEO of the world's most powerful company.

> "Follow your dreams. Do that thing which motivates you from inside and you are passionate about, success will follow you for sure."
>
> —SUNDAR PICHAI

I remember using AOL as my first Internet browser. Yes, AOL. Maybe you remember them too. To help you recall, this was when you couldn't use the phone at the same time you were browsing the Internet; we've come a long way since then. At that time, I didn't think there would be a day where we could actually have an Internet browser that was fast and reliable. Luckily, there were those who did and helped create it; this is why we have that luxury today.

PART 2

THE PRINCIPLES OF ACTION

CHAPTER 4

IMPORTANCE OF BOLDNESS

"Often, in the real world, it's not the smart that get ahead but the bold."

—ROBERT KIYOSAKI

"Be passionate and bold. Always keep learning. You stop doing useful things if you don't learn."

—SATYA NADELLA

Usually, I only venture into downtown for very special events. Luckily, this happened to be the first day of a multiday event filled with guests from all around the world, executives, and several mayors. I gladly braved the cold and stormy weather for this event. Rushing, I didn't want to miss our special guest, the mayor, and not just any mayor but the mayor of Sacramento. As I walked down the long flight of stairs, he was there. I was so nervous that I did not immediately greet him and went my merry way to check in my things. Luckily, one of my new friends showed up, who just so happens to be one of the boldest people I have ever met. So bold that I even got bolder! Then off we went to meet the mayor. I learned an important lesson that day, boldness is contagious.

OVERCOMER

At what age can you conquer your fears and learn to become a bolder person? The answer is: at any age. This lesson can be seen in the lives of the top leaders of today. One of those leaders is Jack Dorsey. He was so shy as a child that he would barely speak at all, not even to his family, because of the speech impediment he had. Then it hit him. He had to conquer this fear, so, he took speech therapy and joined a speech team.

Now, he is a much bolder person and is not afraid to speak his mind. He states, "Pick a movement, pick a revolution, and join it" (Hof, 2012). If there is anyone to learn from about the importance of boldness, it is Jack Dorsey. He is the cofounder and CEO of both Square and Twitter, which are two multibillion-dollar companies.

He is now one of the most famous living CEOs today. However, he didn't set out to become a CEO or a public figure; these had arisen out of necessity. By the time he hit his eighteenth birthday, he had already hacked New York City's largest taxi dispatch company and bravely emailed the company's CEO and offered to help fix the issue. The company had surprisingly offered him a job. This new job took Jack to New York where he came up with another idea to share messages with his friends on the Internet. However, he did not yet implement this idea in the real world.

He was born in St. Louis, Missouri, on November 19, 1976 (Jack, 2021). His father was an engineer, and his mother had a coffee store. He had an interest in technology that started at an early age, and he also began programming as a student. He was quiet and intelligent, fascinated by cities as well as what was happening around them. "It's really complex to make something simple…I've always been fascinated by cities and how they work. And I taught myself how to program so I can understand how the city works."

He wanted to see everything the world had to offer. This was one of the reasons that by the age of fifteen, he had written a dispatch software that had been used by taxicab companies for many years (Jack, 2021). Around this time, he also started helping Jim McKelvey, a cofounder of Square, with one of his first companies, Mira. This is when he earned the nickname, "Jack the Genius." He and Jack continue to have an important relationship.

Eventually Jack moved to the technological capital of the world, San Francisco. He had moved there to join his mentor Greg Kidd, and to cofound a new start-up that would allow for the dispatch of taxis, couriers, and emergency services over the Internet. Things were looking up for him, but suddenly he was let go from the company he was working with, which then led him back home to Missouri. During this time Jack had reinvented himself and became immersed in the punk scene and decided to become a licensed massage therapist. But luckily, his innovative mind wanted to keep creating.

"A founder is not a job, it's a role, an attitude. And it's something that can happen again and again and again, and in fact, it has to happen again and again and again, otherwise, we would not move forward."

—JACK DORSEY

Suddenly he met a tech entrepreneur, who had sold the company called Blogger to Google. He and Jack decided to work on a new company called Odeo, which was a podcasting production company. This idea was short lived due to competitors. After a series of setbacks, Jack considered a new idea. This time, the idea would change the world. He wanted to create a company that would allow users to update their status to their Internet connections in an easy way. Within two weeks, he had built a site where users could post short messages of a hundred and forty characters or less, instantly. Jack's drive in this two-week period had provided key momentum for his product, which would become Twitter. Then, on the momentous date of March 21, 2006, Jack released his first tweet which stated, "just setting up my twttr" (Jack, 2021). At the time, he may have never guessed that his first tweet would be sold for $2.9 million dollars, fifteen years later.

Even though it took Twitter about seven years before it became profitable, Jack stayed consistent. Consistency is an important factor in obtaining success. With a new company, there are no guarantees; but like Jack, if you believe in your ability and take consistent action, you can make great progress.

One progress point was that Jack was made the CEO of Twitter. At thirty years old, he was the leader of what was to become one of the world's biggest technology companies of the twenty-first century. He started to take on the role of a corporate executive. However, he had kept an interest in yoga and fashion, which had started conflicting with his responsibilities. This led to his cofounder replacing him as CEO and moving him over to be a chairman of Twitter's board. Now for the first time ever, Jack had to defend himself.

Jack spoke up about being let go from Twitter by making his disapproval of the issue public. He also went on and created a new company called Square to, in a way, get even. This financial services and digital payments company became successful as well, and now Jack proved himself to be an effective CEO. During this time, in 2013, Twitter had gone public and Jack was now a billionaire.

In 2015, he had found himself once again the CEO of Twitter. Now, he was the CEO of two of the most powerful tech companies in the world. He describes both his companies as utilities that an individual or an organization of any size can pick up and use immediately.

Jack Dorsey has become a phenomenon. When he sees a problem, he is not afraid to fix it. He has been innovating and creating since he was a child. If he would have stopped, we wouldn't have the companies that he has created today. He was also not afraid to start things he knew nothing about, and he has given us the lesson of the importance of beginning what you've been wanting to start, even if it's small at first. "The greatest lesson that I learned in all of this is that you have to start. Start now, start here, and start small. Keep it simple" (Jack, n.d.).

Bold is defined as: courageous and daring; *a bold hero*. Sometimes…we need to be our own hero.

As a bold person, Jack Dorsey is someone who takes action. Even if done in the politest way. Being bold is going out of your comfort zone and doing things you have almost no experience in. Like Jack, other leaders have also started out young and alone in their respective position. One such leader is Sara Blakely.

GET A YES

Sara Blakely is an entrepreneur and the founder of Spanx. She was named the world's youngest, self-made female billionaire by *Forbes* Magazine in March 2012, as well as one of *TIME*'s 100 Most Influential People. Her mission is "to help women feel great about themselves and their potential" (Spanx, n.d.).

Sara had initially planned to become an attorney but had started selling fax machines door-to-door in her late twenties. She was young and energetic, but also frustrated. "I kept feeling like I'm in the wrong movie. You know, like, where's the director? Where's the—where's the producer? This is not my movie. And I was really determined to create a better life for myself" (NPR, 2016). This was when she came up with a brilliant product idea unexpectedly, while getting ready for a party. She had cut the feet out of a control top pantyhose to look better in her white pants. It worked. She liked how it felt and looked under her clothing. At that moment she thought, "This should exist for women."

She had never taken a business class or worked in fashion or retail before, but she went on a mission to create her product. With only $5,000 in savings, she started making calls to hosiery mills to help create her product. She tried for several months but was unable to get their approval. At the same time she was trying to connect with these hosiery mills to help make her product, she was contacting patent attorneys to patent her idea. She wanted to work with a female patent attorney, because she thought it would make it easier to explain her product. But she was not able to find a female patent attorney, because there was no female attorney in the whole state of Georgia at the time.

Staying persistent, Sara took her lucky red backpack, and met with three different law firms that she found online. She had noticed at one of the meetings that one of the attorneys had kept looking around the room during her presentation. Later, she found out that the attorney had thought her idea was so bad that she must have been sent by Candid Camera, a show that featured practical jokes. She had decided after these meetings that she was going to write her own patent. She went to a bookstore and bought the book, *Patents and Trademarks*, which helped her start writing her patent.

At the time Sara was working as a saleswoman selling fax machines door-to-door, where at times she would feel defeated. She would then drive around in her car before her sales pitches just to convince herself to be able to do them. One day, Sara took a week off work, and drove to North Carolina to visit the hosiery mills that she was trying to contact over the phone, trying to convince them to help her make her product. This did not seem to work, and she went back to Atlanta, Georgia. Two weeks after returning from the trip, a mill owner called her and said, "Sara, I have decided to help make your crazy idea" (NPR, 2016). This was a huge break for Sara. She was a single, young woman making a product in a male-dominated arena. The mill owner had run the idea by his daughters who had approved of it, so he agreed to help Sara. Sara's persistence and belief in her idea had been confirmed.

Now Sara had to make the prototype. While spending a year on making the prototype, Sara was wondering, "Where are the women? Why am I not speaking to any women here?" (Inc., 2012). Then it dawned on her that the reason why pantyhose had been so uncomfortable for so long was because the people making them weren't wearing them; or if they were, they weren't admitting it. Also, she found out that when the industry was making the product, they had taken the same size waistband and put them on every pair, no matter what size difference.

With all the information she was learning about the industry, she was making sure to use it to her advantage in the creation of her product. When she was finally able to complete her entire patent, she realized she needed to finish the legal claims portion of it. To her benefit, she had her patent attorney agree to do it even while not fully understanding her idea, but he had seen her passion for it and agreed to do it regardless.

As the patent attorney was creating the legal claims portion of the patent, he didn't know exactly what Sara's product was made from and needed to speak with someone directly at the mill her product was being made in. They were able to speak to a contact there with a deep Southern accent and had obtained the information they needed, which sounded like "70 percent nylon and 30 percent lacquer." At the time, Sara was content with the response she received.

The very night before, however, when Sara was supposed to submit her patent to the US Patent and Trademark Office, she was not able to sleep because she was wondering how there was lacquer in her product. The next morning, Sara took the initiative to call the contact at the mill creating her product and had asked him, "Can you spell lacquer?" He responded with, "Yeah, L-Y-C-R-A."

This spelling check had saved Sara's patent. When Sara told her patent attorney this information, he stated, "Sara, do you know how fast you would've gotten a patent awarded to you on trying to make pantyhose out of paint thinner?" (Inc., 2012). She would have likely obtained one very fast.

Sara was now able to submit her complete patent online and was also finishing up her prototype at the same time. While she waited on the patent response, she was busy making packaging, which had taken her a few months. She knew she wanted it to stand out from the rest and communicate, "I'm new, I'm different; check me out" (Inc., 2012). She did this by making the packaging bright red which, she says, was revolutionary at the time. She had also put three animated, illustrated girls on the front that looked totally different. This was also distinctive because most hosiery packaging had similar photos that hadn't changed in decades.

After she had made the decision on her packaging design, she then turned to more of the legal aspects, which she did not know much about at the time. Many budding entrepreneurs also do not know all the legal aspects of starting a business, but Sara did not let that stop her and decided to navigate this important area in a more eventful way. She figured she would buy ten packages of similar products and if there was matching information on all ten of the packages, then it had to be legal. This is how Sara completed her packaging. Not the most formal way to go about this, but it worked.

The main feature that Sara had yet to decide on was her product's name; one of the best parts of starting a business. She had already spent over a year and a half thinking of names for her product. One of them was "Open-toed Delilahs," which was the runner-up to Spanx. Her theory for the final name came from the idea that the man who started Kodak, named George Eastman, had liked the "k" sound so much that he put the letter at the beginning and the end of his product name, which was one of the most recognized companies in the world at the time. She also knew that the letter "k" makes audiences laugh in the comedy world (Moore, 2021), so she knew she had to include this letter. She had to get this right.

Not long after, while waiting in traffic, she came up with the name, "Spanks." She then got home and decided to change the "k" in the word to "x" because, in her research, she had found out that made-up words were better for products than real words, and it made the trademark process easier as well. She visited the United States Patent and Trademark

Office website and bought her product name and was legally awarded the name.

With the pieces starting to come together, Sara went to her first company to pitch her product. The store was high end and well recognized. Sara had finally connected with a buyer on the phone and was willing to fly to another state to meet with her. When Sara met with the buyer at the company headquarters, she realized, in the middle of her meeting, that she was losing the buyer's interest. This is when she had a brilliant idea.

She immediately asked if she could show the buyer a before and after of her product in real life. What happened next was unexpected. The buyer was bewildered but agreed. Upon seeing the product's before and after on Sara, the buyer was pleased and agreed to place an order for seven stores to see how it sold. The move paid off.

This brought Sara to her next step, which was to advertise her products that were now located in stores. She had decided to pay her friends to buy the products from the seven stores the products were located in. She wanted her products to gain more attention so the buyer will give her another chance. She was also going to the stores herself and demoing the products every day. She realized, however, that her customers still needed a new way to see her product. Being an innovative thinker and risk taker, Sara bought envelope racks to display her products on and then put them next to every cash register at the store where her product was located, even before obtaining approval to do it.

Sometimes you just have to make bold choices.

ONE BOLD MOVE
The next opportunity for Sara came from one bold move and one lucky break. Taking a step of extreme boldness, she sent her product to Oprah. Who would have thought it would become Oprah's favorite product of the year?

Spanx was now being distributed across the world, opening up more opportunities for Sara, such as selling her products on QVC. Even though friends tried to talk her out of selling on QVC, since it was unconventional, Sara went through with the strategy. She ended up selling eight thousand Spanx in five minutes, which is huge.

Sara Blakely had trusted her instincts and turned her dreams into a reality. Her company Spanx was profitable within its first year, and it became a multimillion-dollar company (MasterClass, 2021).

PRACTICE
Being bold can take a while to get accustomed to. When I realized I did not like public speaking I made sure to immerse myself into it head on, even though it was not something I thought I would enjoy. Then I realized that the more I took part in public speaking, the more I got familiar and comfortable with it. Eventually, I learned to have more fun with it and enjoy myself. This was a major milestone because ever since I was a child I was uncomfortable talking in front of an audience. But, after seeing so many great speakers on

stage, I thought it might be useful to get to know how to overcome this and be bolder in terms of speaking in front of an audience.

Some may think that we have to be the loudest in the room or brash to be bold and to stand out, but I see boldness differently. I believe that being bold means putting yourself out there even if you are hesitant.

Being bold helps build the momentum needed to reach greater success; it is not limited by age or the experience you may have. As we have seen with Jack Dorsey and Sara Blakely; it requires bravery to take the action needed to start something new. It may not succeed at first, but having the confidence to continue to make the bold moves needed to make your dreams come true is an important step in the process of achieving great results.

HOW BOLD ARE YOU?

HOW BOLD ARE YOU?

1. When you are at a restaurant, do you order before your guest(s)?

Yes / No

2. When you are experiencing change in your life, do you handle it well?

Yes / No

3. When you need to make a hard decision, do you make the decision right away?

Yes / No

4. When you have a weakness, do you try to strengthen that area?

Yes / No

5. When you have the solution to a problem in your life, do you implement it?

Yes / No

Answers:
Add up the number of times you chose "Yes."
5/5 - Congratulations! You are bold and can possibly teach others on becoming braver.
4/5 - Great! You can do just about anything you set your mind to.
3/5 - Almost there! You have some great moments of boldness but should try to get out of your comfort zone more often.
2/5 - Needs improvement, but with a bit of training, you can also become bold!
1/5 - It's okay! The next time you come across the situations that are presented in this quiz, make sure to take the approach that will help you become bolder. With time, you will improve!

CHAPTER 5

TAKE SMART RISKS

"Someone's sitting in the shade today because someone planted a tree a long time ago."

—WARREN BUFFETT

Have you ever noticed how kids have an easier time taking risks? As we grow, we realize we have more at stake, so we become more careful. However, this same need to be careful can be the reason we hold ourselves back from obtaining something greater. At the same time, we do need to be smart. This is where the value of taking smart risks comes in. But what are "smart risks" exactly, and how do we make them? We make them by calculating our win-to-loss ratio. When we have more gains than losses, it is a smart risk. One of the greatest risk takers in the world teaches this same exact principle.

This risk taker had started his career off on a mission. He even declared to a family friend that he was going to be a millionaire by the time he turned thirty, or he would jump off the tallest building in Omaha (Kennon, 2021). He is none other than Warren Buffett.

As a teenager, Warren took small jobs like most of the teenagers at the time. He also had an interest in business and had started one as a paperboy and had sold horse-racing tip sheets as well. What he did with his earnings was ahead of most of his peers, however. He had used his savings to buy several pinball machines that he then situated in stores (Estevez, 2020). He eventually sold the business, and his senior yearbook picture included the statement: "likes math; a future stockbroker" (Hess, 2018).

Warren Buffett was born in Omaha, Nebraska on August 30, 1930. Known as one of the most successful investors in the world, he is also the chairman and CEO of Berkshire Hathaway, which has the highest-priced publicly traded stock available. When he would visit his father's stock brokerage shop as a child, he would write the stock prices on the blackboard of his office and watch what the shop investors were doing (Warren, 2021). He had shown financial and business capability as a child by the ability to add large columns of numbers in his head.

Warren's start in investing came at an early age. Earlier than you might think. "I made my first investment at age eleven. I was wasting my life up until then" (Warren, 2021). Not long after, he had purchased a stock he believed was undervalued but would have a good return. However, the stock almost lost about a third of its value within a few weeks after he purchased it (Investopedia, 2021). Regardless, he had held onto his stock, and it rebounded, giving him a profitable return when he sold it. After selling it, he watched the stock skyrocket in value to his surprise. This may have been one of the most important life lessons he had ever learned and one he would become famous for in the future: the value of patience.

In 1950, Warren's Harvard Business School application was rejected. He then applied to Columbia due to two of their professors who were well-known security analysts. Warren was accepted.

While there, he read a book by his professor, Benjamin Graham. *The Intelligent Investor* changed his life and set him on the life course of professional analysis to the investment markets (Estevez, 2020). Upon learning one of his professors was on the board of a major insurance company, Warren traveled unannounced to the headquarters to learn more. After his visit, he was so excited, within just a few days, he had spent 65 percent of his $20,000 savings to purchase the insurance company's stock. This stock grew substantially and eventually made Warren the owner of the company (Kennon, 2021). He showed initiative at a very young age.

Eventually, he graduated with his master's degree from Columbia and decided to go to Wall Street. His father and his mentor Ben Graham both advised him against this decision. So, he began selling securities and worked as an analyst. He also bought a Texaco station as a side investment, which did not work out, but Warren kept his entrepreneurial spirit alive.

Around twenty-one years old, he took a Dale Carnegie public speaking course and started to teach a night class at the University of Nebraska called "Investment Principles."

He was now offered an opportunity he could not turn down. It was an offer by Ben Graham, his past mentor, to work at his company, the Graham-Newman Corporation, an investment firm. Two years later, Ben Graham decided to retire.

By now, Warren had accumulated an impressive net worth. However, he still hadn't come close to his goal of having one million dollars by the age of thirty, needing to make over $800,000 in four years to reach his goal. Warren took a leap and formed a firm of his own called Buffett Partnership; within a year, he opened two more partnerships. The very next year, he added two more partnerships again and was now managing five investment partnerships at the age of twenty-seven.

Warren was a millionaire by the age of thirty and achieved his goal, but he did not stop there.

Warren continued investing. At the age of thirty-two, Warren's partnership was now worth $7.2 million (Kennon, 2021), over sixty-two million dollars in today's value. He had grown his investments and had gained valuable experience. This was also the year that he would come across one of his biggest investments yet, Berkshire Hathaway. Warren's company had quickly become the largest shareholder of Berkshire Hathaway. Having invested in several more companies, the Buffett Partnership closed in 1969 after its most successful year. His net worth was now twenty-five million dollars, but this was still the beginning of his career. Warren had achieved great success at this point in his life, but this is where things took a drastic turn.

Unexpectedly, the stock market took one of its biggest hits since the Great Depression in 1974. Warren's net worth had fallen by over 50 percent (Kennon, 2021). This was a big financial loss for him. Yet he did not quit. He continued to invest in more companies. Making smart investments, within ten years, Warren made back more than he had lost during the market crash. His net worth was now at $620 million. When most others gave up, Warren did not. He invested even more, and his risks paid off.

> "Be greedy when others are fearful, and fearful when others are greedy."
>
> —WARREN BUFFETT

He was well on his way to monumental gains, but again, Warren lost half of his personal wealth in 1987 when he was fifty-seven years old. How was he going to make the wealth back at this age? His answer: by investing. He began to buy stocks just two years later in a well-known beverage company for over a billion dollars. This turned out to be one of Warren's most profitable investments to date. His fortune was now at over three billion dollars. Having a personal fortune of three billion dollars did not stop Warren from investing. He continued to invest and has acquired over one hundred billion dollars. He says, "In the world of business, the people who are most successful are those who are doing what they love."

He clearly loves what he does. He not only obtained his childhood goal of becoming a millionaire by the age of thirty, but he surpassed that to become one of the richest people in the world.

Warren Buffett has learned smart strategies that work for him that have resulted in massive rewards. When he takes on risk, he makes sure it is calculated, and this has benefited him greatly.

> *"You do things when the opportunities come along. I've had periods in my life when I've had a bundle of ideas come along, and I've had long dry spells. If I get an idea next week, I'll do something. If not, I won't do a damn thing."*
>
> —WARREN BUFFETT

Studies show that people who enjoy taking risks may be more likely to be content and satisfied with their lives. German researchers surveyed more than twenty thousand people about their risky behavior and found that tall people are more prepared to take risks than short people, women take fewer risks than men, and willingness to take risks decrease dramatically with age. However, I have found that there are techniques that one can apply to overcome these hurdles.

One of these techniques is designed to reduce "brain chatter" by training the brain on being in the present. Whether you're walking, eating, or breathing, focusing on the sights, sounds, and physical sensations of that particular moment can help drown out our habit of replaying mistakes and worries, according to Dr. Tara Swart, a neuroscientist and leadership coach. This strategy, also known as mindfulness, keeps cortisol and adrenaline levels low, which helps with the ability to be clearheaded enough to make intelligent decisions as well as having the ability to take some risks necessary for success in today's ambiguous business world.

Taking smart risks are a key to being successful. Without risks, there is no reward. When you take smart risks, you have the stats in your favor and you are thinking long-term, not just the short-term. Warren Buffett is a prime example of this. He only invests in things that offer good prospects for long-term growth. He also advises to keep your costs minimal and to ignore the chatter: "It is madness to risk losing what you need in pursuing what you simply desire."

"Risk comes from not knowing what you're doing."
—WARREN BUFFETT

GETTING SMARTER WITH RISK

"If you have something that's working; keep on innovating."
—STEPHEN KEY

Stephen Key is an open innovation advocate, licensing expert, author, entrepreneur, and inventRight cofounder. I first heard of Stephen by reading his best-selling book *One Simple Idea* while I was learning about the complex patenting process. When I interviewed him, I would not dream that he had a difficult childhood because of his positive attitude and accolades. He is known as the leading expert on licensing products for passive income and has amazingly patented over twenty products in the last twenty-five years.

As a child, however, Stephen did not have an easy time since he was dyslexic, which he only found out decades later when tested. He was teased but luckily sports had helped him to get on the right path. He had learned to see things differently and to look at things very closely.

Stephen also learned that being a business major in university wasn't the right fit for him and instead took an art class. One day, he went home and told his dad that he wanted to be an artist. He then decided to change his career but when he became an actual art student, he had the realization that wasn't the right place for him either. He decided that was going to be a hard way to make a living. So, he started to make things by hand and sell them at fairs for seven years. He realized he liked to make things that were quick and easy.

One of his creations happened to be a stuffed tomato as well as other vegetable toys he called Softies. He learned very important lessons back then; if it didn't sell, then come up with something very quick. One of his products that had hit big and changed everything was a rotating spin label. The rotating spin label is two labels in one; the top label spins around the container and reveals what is printed on the base label through a clear window (Spinformation, 2021). He knew he hit something big the moment he made it. Even though the rotating spin label was rejected over a hundred times, he kept trying to grow it.

At one point, he was told that the idea of his rotating spin label was not new and that it was invented fifty years ago. As well as he would never get a patent on it. He was told to "forget about it" by his attorney. After this revelation, Stephen read the patents for the rotating spin label, realizing that, to his dismay, he didn't invent it, someone else had. But he also realized there was no method of how to manufacture it at the time. This took him back to the drawing board. He was able to obtain the patent to the manufacturing process and license the product to a very large company that gave him royalties and he sold hundreds of millions of labels (InspiredInsider, 2021). Stephen did not take no for an answer, he found a way to make his idea work.

But eventually, the royalties stopped, and he had to reinvent himself.

At fifty years old, Stephen walked away from the rotating spin label and came up with a new invention: a themed guitar pick. He went all-in with the guitar pick idea, named it HotPicks, and learned what he needed to as he went. When he and his team first came out with a design, they couldn't sell them. The designs were his, and he knew he was wrong.

Stephen then went to study the marketplace, which was a fashion store at a mall. He noticed in one store that there were many skulls everywhere. He was perplexed. He asked himself, "Why are kids buying these skulls?" He then went back and designed a skull guitar pick. When he took it to a trade show, he told his partner, "Why don't we just throw all of these guitar picks on the table?" This created a mob since he was giving them away for free. There were so many people that wanted them, that even the buyers couldn't get to them.

Stephen knew that the skull design was going to work because before he made the product, he wanted to test the market since the mold for the skull guitar pick was going to be $3,000. This was indeed a smart risk since he had put out surveys for his guitar pick designs in multiple music stores. He told the employees if they filled out the surveys, including different design options for guitar picks, he would give them twenty dollars for a stack of the filled-out flyers. Also, anyone else who filled them out would get free guitar picks when he made them.

This plan worked. When picking up the surveys from the music stores, Stephen had noticed that they all picked the skull design. There were multiple designs to choose from, but everyone chose the skull. He had let the market choose what it wanted. "Always listen to your customer" (InspiredInsider, 2021).

One day, Stephen decided to go bigger. He had gone to a local convenience store employee and convinced them to put his display up for a couple of days, except the manager was initially against it. When Stephen went back two days later, the display was gone. He had asked, "Well, how did they do?" Stephen thought they had taken the display away because they didn't do well.

Then the employee replied, "Steve, we sold out of every one. We need more!" This was when Stephen realized that sometimes you just have to do things a little differently. He believes that if he would have gone to the corporate headquarters, they would have said no.

By going to the local store and talking to the manager, he was given an opportunity. The regional manager had even called him and complimented him on his product. They were able to get major distribution with the entire convenience store chain (InspiredInsider, 2021).

Stephen's process of growing his company worked. He had started in a very small niche first, became successful, and then went broader. He expanded his designs and had a guitar pick for every lifestyle. They eventually had sold tens of millions of these guitar picks. Stephen was surprised that "such a simple change to an existing product that's been around forever could create such a passion" (InspiredInsider, 2021). They ultimately became a collector's item.

Out of the blue at a trade show, Stephen received a deal with Walmart. Every entrepreneur wanted their product to be sold by them. Setbacks quickly arose. Before this time, Stephen was not producing the number of products he would have to manufacture in the first order with Walmart.

Stephen realized they would have to scale quickly, needing approximately one hundred people to be able to fulfill the orders that Walmart had placed and wanted within ten days. They currently had only five team members.

Even though Stephen lost a lot of weight from worry during this challenge, he ended up figuring it out. They became the number one best-selling small musical accessory with their girl's rock guitar picks at Walmart, which were designed by his daughter.

Stephen even became an exclusive Disney licensee with his guitar picks. He was selling Mickey Mouse guitar picks and other branded guitar picks as well. He had no idea what was coming next. In a meeting with Disney, his partner said, "Show them that spin label you have." They had interest in the product and helped him to move it forward and into the market once again. Stephen's label had told a story, a perfect match for them to work with.

THE RISKS TO SUCCESS
Stephen has taken many risks. These risks have helped him accomplish what many dream of: being able to create products and sell them successfully. He overcame many roadblocks in his path, even though he could have moved on many times. By taking consistent risks to grow and improve, he became successful. He has now helped entrepreneurs from all over the world license their ideas to thousands of retailers. He has also cofounded the Inventors Groups of America, a nonprofit dedicated to supporting the efforts of inventors' associations across the United States. "I've made all the mistakes and they're not really mistakes; they're stepping stones to success" (InspiredInsider, 2021).

If Stephen had not taken risks with his time and investments, then he would not have been able to help touch lives all around the world through the inventions and products he has sold, which amount to more than half a billion units.

He was able to gain the experience he needed as he went along, and because of this was able to learn how to take smarter risks and teach others how to take smarter risks as well.

Take Walt Disney for example. When we picture what he has created, we picture fun and a good time. How could you picture anything else when you think of the Disney enterprise? His legacy, however, was full of risks which started as a child. He realized then that he had an interest in drawing and decided to build upon this by taking art classes. By taking these classes, he was able to get better at his skills and learn more about his craft. One of the most important skills he learned was to take risks which he then tested and executed. This foundation was what he was able to build his dreams on and went onto produce more than one hundred feature films and has won one hundred and thirty-five Academy Awards with thirty-two being won personally and is in the *Guinness Book of World Records*. He learned to take smart risks with the use of testing and then by also putting his plans into action. Through this process, he was able to make his dreams into a reality.

"*I dream, I test my dreams against my beliefs, I dare to take risks, and I execute my vision to make those dreams come true.*"

—WALT DISNEY

Taking smart risks requires taking the time to do the research to find out what the best strategy is. This time spent can help reap great rewards in the future. Smart risks are what has built Silicon Valley and Wall Street in the first place and will continue to be a driving force in the world.

SMART RISK ASSESSMENT

Smart Risk Assessment

1. Before making an important decision, do you get reputable advice first?

Yes / No

2. When taking risks, do you use money that you can afford to lose?

Yes / No

3. Do you have more than one stream of income?

Yes / No

4. Do you make sure to learn new skills often?

Yes / No

5. Are you open to new ways of doing things?

Yes / No

Answers:
Add up the number of times you chose "Yes."
5/5 - Congratulations! You know how to take smart risks and should continue to make even more.
4/5 - Great! You have learned how to take most risks in a smart and capable manner.
3/5 - Almost there! You have taken some smart risks but should try to do more research on smart risks.
2/5 - Needs improvement, but with the right amount of knowledge, you can improve your risk-taking ability!
1/5 - It's time to do some important research and then put smart risk-taking strategies into place!

CHAPTER 6

KEEP CREATING

How many times have you wanted to create something but got too busy? Being creative is an important step to figuring out what makes us who we are.

When I spoke with Ryan Tedder, the lead singer of OneRepublic, I was astonished at how many things he has created outside of music. He is known to have created many hit songs for himself as well as hit songs for others, such as "Halo" by Beyoncé, "Rumour Has It" by Adele, and many more. He is a major hit maker, which most of us already know. However, what most may not know is that he is a serial entrepreneur. I wanted to know what piece of advice had helped him the most and his response was, "You just have to take the first step and then you take another one and another one, eventually, you're in a full-on sprint and that's really the best advice I could give."

Having created many different things throughout my life, I see how this has helped me to grow and to be able to notice more of the possibilities that exist in this world. Now as an adult, I realize we need to continue to keep creating to be able to keep progressing. In an inspiring talk with the inventor of the cell phone, Martin Cooper, he told me about a paper that he had just written on the importance of learning. He said if you don't keep learning your whole life, there's not much reason to keep living, and if you stop learning, you lose the ability to learn. I find this fascinating because I have found that through creating I am also able to learn.

"Learning is like a muscle. If you don't use your muscles, they atrophy, and you can't recover them. So, I think that learning is a lifelong thing."
—MARTIN COOPER

"Today we do what others won't, so that tomorrow we can accomplish what others can't."
—ROBERT HERJAVEC

One of the most well-known creators we have today is Robert Herjavec. Robert Herjavec is known as one of the original sharks on the hit series show *Shark Tank*. We all may know of his successful track record, but did you know he had a very tough beginning? He was born on September 14, 1962, in Yugoslavia (present-day Croatia) in a small village named Zbjeg, which translates to "flee" in English. The village was named this because it was a small town that people would come to during the many wars. His upbringing included his father having been taken by the communist regime twenty-two times for being an anticommunist. To escape communism, his family finally fled to Halifax, Nova Scotia, with only a single suitcase. After first trying unsuccessfully to get into the US, they were able to make it to Canada, where they lived in a friend's basement for eighteen months. He had a tough childhood, but he learned many important lessons from it.

One of the lessons was to never complain. "Nothing pisses me off more than when people complain," he states (Robert, 2017). Robert during childhood had much to complain about as it was not easy being a new immigrant in Canada. One day after coming home crying and venting to his mom about being bullied, his father had heard him and gave him an important lesson which he still follows to this day which was to never complain.

From here on out, he was a creator, not a complainer.

In 1984, Robert graduated from the University of Toronto with a degree in English literature and political science. He believes he made the right choice. "The ability to communicate is fundamental to what I do" (Cassell, 2019). He then went on to jobs that are completely different than what he does today. To support his family, he waited tables, delivered newspapers, and became a retail salesman and debt collector. He even went into the film industry for a short time as an assistant director. These jobs were not satisfying, and Robert did something that most individuals don't do but should. He applied for a position at a company he wasn't qualified for and convinced the company to give him the position there by working for free. This worked out well and he rose to the general manager role.

Yet, he got fired.

Immediately after this, he started his own company from his basement. The company was called BRAK Systems, which was a Canadian integrator of Internet security software. In March 2000, Robert was offered $30.2 million for the company by AT&T Canada. "I was one of those guys who never wanted to start their own business. I never saw myself as a leader. I saw myself as a great number two. I just wanted to do a good job and make a little more money every year" (Lagorio, 2012).

He continued growing his career after this successful acquisition to become the Vice President of Sales at Ramp Network, which was then sold for $225 million to Nokia. After a few years, he created his biggest company yet, The Herjavec Group, an IT integrator that does computer security and information storage for enterprise and government. It had soon become one of North America's fastest-growing technology companies. "I'm not selling this one. Not for a long, long time. I'm really inspired to build a billion-dollar company" (Lagorio, 2012).

After doing well in the business world, Robert had received the opportunity to be on a show in Canada called *Dragon's Den* in 2006. This caused him to be a household name. Three years later, Robert also became a *Shark Tank* star, which has now won four Emmys. He is known on the show as the "Nice Shark." After all his success, Robert still stays humble, and that is important. "Humility is more effective than arrogance" (Robert, 2021).

It's hard to predict where a person will be in the next five years, but one thing is for sure. If a person keeps creating, they will gain the experience they need to build momentum. Like with Robert, opportunities will show up and you can build the skills needed for a successful finish.

"A goal without a timeline is just a dream."
—ROBERT HERJAVEC

Most of the top companies of today were focused on completely unrelated products and/or services. This is hard to imagine, but landing on a successful business venture takes quite a bit of pivoting. One of these examples is Amazon. Amazon first focused on books. When they started doing this well, they added even more types of products to their company. Another example of this is McDonald's. In 1927, siblings Dick and Mac McDonald opened a hot dog stand together, which they called "The Airdrome" in an airport in California. It was twenty-one years later that the company had started to focus on the hamburgers they became known for.

It is easy to get carried away by the thought of creating something new. However, it is important to also make sure what we create will have a positive impact on the world. The more useful things we create, the more potential for success it will have. Benjamin Franklin throughout his life invented many products, but he was most known for the discovery of electricity. He did this by using his creativity. He flew a kite during a thunderstorm and tied a metal key to the kite string to conduct it.

He had accomplished his goal, but not without getting shocked! Luckily, he lived and continued to create the lightning rod to protect people, buildings, and ships from lightning. Then he went on to have his image appear on the US hundred-dollar bill: the largest valued bill in circulation, and to this day he continues to appear on it, even hundreds of years later. Benjamin's discovery of electricity led others such as Thomas Edison to also create their own inventions that have helped to better society, such as the light bulb.

What would we do without the light bulb?

"The best way to predict the future is to create it."
—ABRAHAM LINCOLN

One of the top creators of our time is Jeff Bezos. Jeff Bezos is the CEO and founder of one of the top companies in the world, Amazon. He is also the founder of the aerospace manufacturer and suborbital spaceflight services company, called Blue Origin. While we may have seen Amazon's rise through the years, we may have never actually learned all the behind-the-scenes work and time that it took to get there.

Jeff Bezos was born on January 12, 1964, in New Mexico. As a toddler, he had actually taken apart his crib with a screwdriver because he wanted to sleep in a real bed. His mother remarried when Jeff was only a few years old and was adopted by his stepfather who changed Jeff's last name to Bezos. It wasn't until Jeff was ten years old before he had found out his stepfather was not his birth father.

Jeff had many interests growing up, one of which included space. He had told a teacher, "The future of mankind is not on this planet" (Carlson, 2011). He may have been right. His dreams of becoming a space entrepreneur have come true with the creation of his space company, Blue Origin.

However, as a teen, he had to start from humble beginnings. Having an interest in technology, he was able to rig an electric alarm to keep his siblings out of his room. Even with such talent, he worked a normal teenage job one summer where he decided to create a summer camp instead. He has always had a creative mind and was not scared to start new initiatives even then. He continued to keep his space dreams alive as a teenager; and at the age of eighteen he stated he wanted "to build space hotels, amusement parks and colonies for two million or three million people who would be in orbit. 'The whole idea is to preserve the earth,' he told a newspaper…The goal was to be able to evacuate humans. The planet would become a park" (Neate, 2018).

After high school, he attended the prestigious Princeton University where he graduated with highest honors in computer science and electrical engineering. After graduation, he worked on Wall Street in the computer science department. He continued climbing the career ladder and became vice president at Bankers Trust. He was working for a hedge fund when he found out that web usage was growing at 2,300 percent a year, so he decided he would find a business plan that made sense to him growth-wise. To decide, he made a list of the top twenty products he could sell on the Internet. He decided on books; "in the book space there are over three million different books worldwide active in print at any given time across all languages, more than 1.5 million in English alone. So, when you have that many items you can literally build a store online that couldn't exist any other way" (Hamilton, 2021).

To follow his dreams, Jeff left his stable career to work on his start-up idea. He even joked that he wanted to have a garage start-up story like Silicon Valley legends from Hewlett-Packard. He did just that. Jeff moved to Seattle because of its reputation as a tech hub and financed the company with the help of his parents who had used their life savings. "And you know, that was a very bold and trusting thing for them to do because they didn't know. My dad's first question was, 'What's the Internet?' Okay. So, he wasn't making a bet on this company or this concept. He was making a bet on his son, as was my mother. So, I told them I thought there was a 70 percent chance that they would lose their whole investment, which was a few hundred thousand dollars, and they did it anyway" (Carter, 2020).

Thankfully, the company started to grow fast. By May 15, 1997, only three years after launching, it went public. Two years later, Amazon had surpassed its competitors. When the dotcom crash came not long after, analysts started calling the company "Amazon.bomb." Still, the company was one of the few able to get through this hard time successfully.

Jeff continued to grow Amazon and with witty ideas has continued to outpace competitors. He has added many features to Amazon and now has grown it to an entire marketplace, one he planned from the beginning. He had originally named the company Amazon because it was known as the earth's largest river, and he was building the world's largest bookstore. "This is not only the largest river in the world;

it's many times larger than the next biggest river. It blows all other rivers away" (Clifford, 2019).

Amazon had grown so rapidly that it surpassed Walmart in 2015 as the most valuable retailer in the United States by market capitalization. Exactly as Jeff wanted. Even as Amazon became one of the top five technology companies in the world and he has become one of the richest people in the world holding the number one spot several times, he continues to create.

Jeff has created a successful company through continuing to create and he does not seem to be slowing anytime soon. As his company has touched most of our lives in some way or another, we can be sure that it has transformed how many people shop online. I am always surprised when my orders arrive as fast as they do since this is the only company able to do so. I applaud his work and the ability to go after his dreams. After conquering the business world on Earth, he is getting ready to conquer space. "When it comes to space, I see it as my job; I'm building infrastructure the hard way. I'm using my resources to put in place heavy lifting infrastructure so the next generation of people can have a dynamic, entrepreneurial explosion into space" (Knapp, 2016).

Being a pioneer is not new to Jeff, nor is it easy. With humble beginnings he pursued his passions and has built very productive companies throughout the years. By continuing to create, he is accomplishing many record-breaking innovations. If we learn anything from Jeff, it would be to learn as you go and to keep creating to obtain higher chances of success.

"What we need to do is always look into the future."
—JEFF BEZOS

Robert Herjavec and Jeff Bezos are both very creative individuals, as most already know, but what most don't know is they both were able to create great companies from humble beginnings. When things looked difficult for them, they did not stop; they continued to create, which is why they have become experts in their fields.

CREATING ASSESSMENT

Creating Assessment

1. Have you thought about working on a new goal recently?
   Yes / No

2. Do you ever learn about how something is made?
   Yes / No

3. Are you good at starting a project?
   Yes / No

4. Are you also good at finishing a project?
   Yes / No

5. Have you been complimented on anything that you have created?
   Yes / No

Answers:
Add up the number of times you chose "Yes."
5/5 - You are a creative powerhouse! Continue to inspire others with your work.
4/5 - Great! You can create things with ease.
3/5 - Almost there. If you push yourself to be creative, your abilities will grow.
2/5 - It's okay. You can improve with practice.
1/5 - Try again when you have implemented new creative strategies, and watch your score grow!

CHAPTER 7

TRYING THINGS IN A SHORT PERIOD OF TIME

"Move fast and break things. Unless you are breaking stuff, you are not moving fast enough."

—MARK ZUCKERBERG

"People think innovation is just having a good idea but a lot of it is just moving quickly and trying a lot of things."

—MARK ZUCKERBERG

Trying things in a short period of time may sound daunting, but it is much better than being delayed.

We may delay starting something before we ever begin it. This is usually due to overthinking. However, perfection cannot be obtained until there is a canvas to work with. Once you have something that you can improve on, that is when the process starts. We see this being put into practice on many occasions by creative individuals, Mark Zuckerberg being one of them.

Mark Zuckerberg has an unusual story on how he became the CEO and cofounder of Facebook. Born on May 14, 1984, in New York, he always had a knack for trying things and at a fast pace as well. When Mark was eleven, he started learning Atari BASIC Programming from his father who then hired a tutor to continue to teach him. About two years later, Mark had already created a computer network called ZuckNet for his family to allow the computers in their home and his father's dental office to communicate. He then started to develop computer games including a computer version of Monopoly and a version of Risk set in the Roman Empire as well. With his new skills, he took off.

Mark started to create even more ideas. One of his next ventures was writing a music player called Synapse Media Player. This used artificial intelligence to learn the user's listening habits and recommend other music. When he posted it online to the AOL platform, it received thousands of positive reviews. That was amazing for a teenager. Then Microsoft and AOL offered to buy his project Synapse for one million dollars as well as hire him as a developer. At such a young age, he surprisingly did not accept and decided to enroll at Harvard University in September 2002 instead (Bellis, 2019).

While attending Harvard University, he studied psychology and computer science. Both subjects had become very important to his future initiatives. He continued to create a program, and this time it was for making class selection decisions based on the choices of other students and also to help them form study groups, called Course Match (Bellis, 2019). He always had a knack for creating solutions to problems and trying things in short periods of time.

He quickly moved on to another idea. It was a program with the stated purpose of finding out who was the most attractive person on campus, called FaceMash. This had been successful but gained controversy particularly with women's groups and he ended the project. Again, in usual fashion, he moved on to a new idea.

This time, it would be his biggest hit.

It was called TheFacebook. It intended to be a reliable directory based on real information about the students at Harvard. It allowed them to use their ".edu" email addresses and photos to connect with other students at the school (McFadden, 2020). This led to the launch of what we know as Facebook today, in February 2004. Within only twenty-four hours of the launch, about 1,200 students had signed up to the platform. In one month, already around half of Harvard undergraduates had a profile. (McFadden, 2020). It started to grow even more and was being used in other schools.

Mark moved fast to grow it. He renamed it "Facebook" after buying the domain name for a whopping $200,000 in 2005. It was so costly because the previous owner knew the domain name was now in high demand. The company started growing rapidly and attracted major investors. Mark decided to move to San Francisco to grow his company. Within a year, he expanded Facebook to include a version for high school students. He knew it was time to quickly expand even further.

In September 2006, the company announced that anyone who was at least thirteen years old and had a valid email address could join (McFadden, 2020). Within two years, he had created it into a platform used worldwide. To continue to keep Facebook relevant, Mark has not been hesitant to try new features for his company. The best move he has made is the acquisition of Instagram, which cost the company one billion dollars in 2012. Instagram is now worth over one hundred and ten billion dollars, an increase in about one hundred and nine billion dollars in a little over nine years. Quite the improvement.

It is better to try things in a short period of time than wait. The reason is we may never truly know when the right timing will be until we have the experience. This way we can be fully prepared when opportunity comes. By trying things in a short amount of time, Mark was able to not only develop his skills but further learn what he was capable of. At the age of twenty-three, he had become the world's youngest billionaire.

"You are better off trying something and having it not work and learning from that than not doing anything at all."

—MARK ZUCKERBERG

CLARITY IN THE JOURNEY

In my twenties, I made it a point to try many different career paths. I wanted to learn which one I would like the best. While doing so, I learned what many find out too late: things are not always how they appear. However, trying things in a short period of time has helped me narrow my goals into better choices because I had gained experience in them.

Now, instead of having regrets, I have clarity.

We do not have to overwork ourselves when we try to achieve things in a short period of time, however. According to studies, we are at our most productive when we break big projects down into smaller chunks and plan a recovery period right after (Ciotti, 2014).

At the age of thirty-six, a man named Jonny Kim had become a US Navy lieutenant and a Navy SEAL, Harvard-trained physician, and NASA astronaut preparing to go to the moon. He was also married with children. Jonny could have stopped at one of these accomplishments since even holding one of these is considered the top of the career ladder, but Jonny had the urge and confidence to go after all of his dreams. He did not let his age or the amount of time it would take define what he wanted to accomplish. He went after his goals and accomplished a tremendous amount because he took action. He tried things in a short period of time and now he can not only defend our country at the highest level, but he can also help save lives with his medical expertise and help advance civilization into space with his NASA training and exploration. "I didn't have a lot of confidence growing up[...] but trying new things, things that I was scared of, made me realize that we are all so much stronger than we give ourselves credit for" (Jonny, 2020).

Imagine what we all could accomplish if we took the barriers off what we think we could do and try more things.

"A lot of opportunities you only get once."

—SHAWN FLYNN

Shawn Flynn is the founder and host of the podcast *The Silicon Valley Podcast* and investment banker at Global Capital Markets. Being a native of Silicon Valley, he has seen it grow into the technology hub it is today. However, growing up, he was monitored a lot since he was the first baby born after his mother received an experimental heart valve replacement. His mother had to continue to have a new heart valve replacement every twelve years. Even with this difficult situation, Shawn continued to participate in regular activities such as sports, which he excelled at, especially in martial arts.

Little did he know how martial arts would help him in the future and in a very unexpected way…

At the age of seven, he learned an important lesson, one he still remembers today. While at his father's pharmacy where he was helping like he did on many occasions; he looked out of a window and noticed a brand new, shiny BMW being driven into their parking lot. Even as a child, he knew that it had to be an expensive car. He noticed how the gentlemen who owned the car also had on a gold watch, suit, and tie. To Shawn, this man looked like he was a billionaire—on top of the food chain, so to speak. After his father sold the gentlemen his medicine, he turned around and told Shawn the man was going to be dead in six months. Shawn was shocked. As a young boy, this was surprising to him. His father went on to explain to him that the medicine he had given the man is not taken unless it's the "end."

Shawn had learned a very important lesson that day and one he still has not forgotten. Appearances can be deceiving. He also found out on that day that life is short, and he had to experience it on a greater degree.

After graduating from the University of San Diego, he went to Costa Rica and realized it was a world away from Silicon Valley where he had grown up. A few months turned into two years. Shawn was enamored with the culture. He had never experienced anything like it before and immersive learning became his focus. He was learning to salsa dance and speak Spanish, what many dream of. After this experience, Shawn was even more interested in international travel. This time, he wanted to challenge himself even more. He went to one of the hardest countries to immigrate to: China (World Population Review, n.d.).

An intended one-year journey here quickly turned into five on and off. Shawn started building companies with one becoming a success. Starting a company in China is not easy, especially if you do not know how to speak the language well, but being determined, Shawn made it work. He noticed a specific need in the country, which was foreign language teachers for children, and started a company to fulfill it. There was plenty of opportunity for his burgeoning company. Shawn was now staffing teachers to the universities that needed them and then expanded this to staffing extras in movies as well as to voice development and software companies.

He became the go-to person in Beijing to connect companies to foreign talent.

There was such a great need for native English speakers that Shawn's company thrived. However, Shawn's father had passed amid his company's growth, so he had to come back to the US to help support his mother and two sisters. His father did not have a will at the time, so the family had to support each other until they could organize everything. In that time, Shawn had to find a source of income fast. The profits he received from his company in China did not convert well to US dollars. He thought, "What can I do to have a flexible job, that I can help my mom and take care of all these things, but I can come and go at any time?" His options were real estate or personal training. He realized real estate would take too long to generate sales in, so he ultimately chose personal training since he already had martial arts experience.

Shawn started making connections and eventually his clients gave him referrals to work at their companies. However, looking at his resume, the companies all told him that he would get bored and leave, even with his skills in foreign languages, contracts, and negotiations, as well as a degree in mechanical engineering. Shawn didn't understand their concept since most of the workers in Silicon Valley did not stay in a position for long anyways.

After meeting with several angel investors, things started to finally move forward.

There were many factors to Shawn's success. He credits much of his success to being located in Silicon Valley, as well as saying yes to opportunities. These opportunities helped him try things in a short period of time where he learned valuable skills. Since Shawn gained these valuable skills, he now works with institutions, governments, and various capital sources to help promote economic growth on a global scale. He is also heavily involved in the Silicon Valley technology ecosystem of fast-growing and high-potential businesses.

"When you say yes to things they lead to other things. And then those other things lead to other things and it's when you say no and you block yourself off, momentum stops."

—SHAWN FLYNN

Our past skills can accumulate and serve us in the future. Just like with the cofounder of Apple, Steve Jobs. He had acquired a broad set of skills that did not make any sense together. Eventually, Steve used those very same skills to create a product that changed the world.

Similarly, in a group meeting I had with Steve Wozniak, the cofounder of Apple, it was the same teaching. He had developed skills that at the time didn't seem relevant, but the same skills became highly coveted years later when technology took off.

Trying things in a short period of time can help us to learn more about the world and our likes and dislikes, which can help serve us in the future. When we allow ourselves to try new things, we not only grow, but we develop new skills that many others may not have at the moment but may need, which can put us in a great position.

CHAPTER 8

RAPID LEARNERS

"Tell me and I forget, teach me and I may remember, involve me and I learn."

—BENJAMIN FRANKLIN

I hear one of the loudest roars from a car I have ever heard. Frantically, I try to remember how I was actually supposed to drive this thing—this thing that's worth the price of a house. I remind my friend to put on her seat belt as I try not to picture her flying out of the car if something unexpected happens. I think she was also shocked at the loud sound of this beast. I was not ready, but we had to go. As I started driving, I could feel the horsepower of this car; it was a racing car and was definitely living up to it. I kept calm and wondered what I would do if something were to happen, but there was really no time to think—only to react to what I was taught just five minutes prior. Questions raced through my mind. Is this the way I'm going to die? What did I get myself into? Why are we headed toward a busy road?

Well, this was how I learned to drive my very first super car. Would I do it again? Yes, and I have. Would I do it again the same way? No—I was scared. If I could do it all over again, I would take more time learning beforehand all the new maneuvers I had to know for this unique car. However, I did just fine. That is the power of learning on the go as well as learning fast for the sake of safety.

A study found that some individuals learn faster because they find learning more rewarding and not actually because they are smarter (Dartmouth, n.d.). This is surprising because we tend to believe smarter individuals learn faster. However, this study shows that individuals who may have more of an interest in what they are learning can have the ability to learn faster than someone who does not have a natural interest in what they are learning. "Basically, you can have two people of identical IQ, but one will get a bigger innate reward signal when they get an answer correct than others, so they'll tend to learn faster not because they are smarter, but because they find it more rewarding," states Peter Tse, professor in Dartmouth's Department of Psychological and Brain Sciences (Dartmouth, n.d.).

I have always learned the fastest by doing things. It is one of the best ways to learn. It also helps with achieving the coveted "flow state," which is when we stop thinking and get into the zone. This flow is associated with subjective well-being, satisfaction with life, and general happiness. At work, it's linked to productivity, motivation, and company loyalty (Robb, 2019).

One example of flow for me is when I write. The most creative and interesting pieces of work have come from when I was in this "flow state." It does not come automatically but when

I do get into a flow state, it is a very uplifting experience. Fortunately, there are ways to help us get into the flow state more often. One is getting away from distractions, like noise and movement. This can seem difficult at first, but if we listen to the wise words of Ray Zinn, it can be done.

Ray Zinn is the longest-serving CEO in Silicon Valley. Upon hearing the title "the longest-serving CEO in Silicon Valley," one might be intimidated. Luckily, Ray believes in treating people with respect, and it is one of the very ideals he lives by. Speaking with Ray, I learned a lot. As someone who has worked for over thirty-seven years in one of the most influential areas of the world, Silicon Valley, he knows what he is doing.

He was born in El Centro, California, on September 24, 1937. His lessons started at an early age; being the oldest of eleven children, he had to learn very fast since he had to help take care of his siblings. One of these lessons came when he was four when he was entrusted to go grocery shopping by himself. These days, many wouldn't dream of letting a four-year-old go to the grocery store by themselves, but Ray showed capability even then. He was able to learn rapidly and get what was needed done.

He continued this practice as he grew. When he was thirteen, he was able to acquire a driver's license. He also was working by then and provided for himself through a paper route. Ray was self-sufficient as a teenager. Growing up on a ranch had given him a sense of responsibility. "I developed a very strong work ethic at a very young age[…]having to go collect money from my customers, and of course, the responsibility of delivering them every day. That really was a hallmark of how I got to where I am."

Ray grew his sense of responsibility and work ethic early. It was also necessary. "If I wanted to enjoy something, I had to get my chores out of the way quickly and early. And so, I just learned to do things I didn't want to do first, get them out of the way, and then the rest of the day became more productive."

This served him well into his adult years. Ray started and funded his own company, Micrel, with his own savings and a bank loan. As other companies took venture capital investments, Ray decided he wanted control of his destiny and chose to not take any venture capital investment. This worked well since his company was profitable from the very first year.

Lately, we have been hearing of many CEOs in Silicon Valley treating their employees unfairly, but not Ray. "Our culture was honesty, integrity, respect for every individual, and then doing whatever it takes, no excuses." He learned this was important to running a healthy company, which is proved by his company having had the lowest employee turnover in the semiconductor industry.

Another lesson Ray learned is communication. After losing his eyesight during his company's IPO, he had to convince his board of directors that he could continue to run his company. He was able to convince them and ran his company for another twenty years. "In the larger scheme of things, I certainly did not want to have to learn how to navigate the world sightless, it was hard and required I change my way of communicating; I would have preferred to have my sight back. But I played the hand I was dealt, and I stuck with it and learned new ways of navigating the world because being able to continue to run Micrel was the goal" (Knyszewski, 2021).

The most important lesson that Ray learned and is known for is "do the tough things first." A rare habit to many, but a useful one. "When you master tasks and skills that you used to dread and hate even, you not only become proficient at those tasks, but you learn to love what you once hated. In order to grow and lead, you must master a wide variety of skills, especially those you dislike."

Running his own multinational company was no easy task, but through his ability to learn rapidly as he went, Ray succeeded. He was able to sell his company for $839 million and continues to be involved in the community through his national ZinnStarter program, which provides both the financial and mentoring support for students to launch new products and companies (ZinnStarter, 2018).

LEAP OF FAITH

Programs such as Ray Zinn's ZinnStarter are crucial for those who would like to learn more about entrepreneurship. Entrepreneurs have to compete in an ever-evolving world. With the sheer amount of competition and technological advances to keep updated on, programs such as these can help give entrepreneurs the ability to keep up.

When I signed on to my first entrepreneurial program, I knew it was going to be an interesting experience since I would have to learn to create a company in a span of only fifty-four hours. This was a big learning experience. Not only did I learn to work well in a team, but I also learned to communicate better. I thought I could communicate well before this, but nothing prepares you better than a high-pressure atmosphere where you have to learn discipline quickly.

Companies are some of the greatest examples of needing to learn fast, YouTube being one of them. Did you know YouTube was originally a video-based dating service? However, that idea did not take off, so the founders pivoted to allow any video to be uploaded to the service, and the rest is history.

When things aren't moving the way you would like, do not be scared to pivot or change.

When we hear about the successes of others, such as Steve Jobs, we think that they have made no mistakes. This is not true. In fact, most success stories also have many difficulties included. Steve Jobs had multiple products that did not work out, yet he concentrated mostly on what did. He learned what worked and what didn't, and moved on. That is what makes the difference.

Creating my first online business, I learned a lot in a short period of time. The list is mind-blowing. Developing an eye-catching website, figuring out which plug-ins to use on the website (there are thousands), finding manufacturers and suppliers, social media development, advertisement. It was a lot. Within a month or two, it was fully functioning. I completed my goal of learning how to build an online store.

You would think that was the end of the story, but along with any business, there was always more to do.

I learned rapidly there is no "hands-off" business, but there is a way to make it easier, which is hiring the right people. Not doing everything is a difficult thing for a business owner. We feel like only we can do things right. These days, you can outsource what you need, meaning hire another person or team to complete tasks. Saving time and energy for the big picture. I realized quickly that some aspects of a business are best outsourced.

MAKING TIME

Making time to grow is the most important thing you can do. In fact, most billionaires read more than the average person. They are usually some of the busiest people in the world, yet they take the time to utilize this hobby. Interestingly, Elon Musk taught himself programming by reading books, and rocket science as well. Knowing he now has an actual rocket company partnered with NASA, that was time well spent.

Reading is a quick way to learn fast. In fact, reading a book was what inspired me to finally become an entrepreneur. I had always wanted to but had not really gone for it. That is until the one fateful day I picked up "the book."

So, which book will you read next?

"*I was raised by books. Books, and then my parents.*"

—*ELON MUSK*

SUMMARY

RAPID LEARNING

1. MAKE TIME TO LEARN
Prioritize time in your schedule to increase knowledge.

2. READ OFTEN
Read educational materials in the form of books, online publications, and magazines.

3. LEARN FROM EXPERIENCE
Learn from those who went before you as well as your own experiences.

4. GET INTO "FLOW STATE"
Remove distractions and make time to think.

CHAPTER 9

TEACHERS AND MENTORS

"A lot of people have gone further than they thought they could because someone else thought they could."

—ZIG ZIGLAR

Teachers and mentors have the capability to change our life dramatically. Then why is it that most of us do not utilize this important resource? Research is very much in favor of having a mentor:

- 71 percent of Fortune 500 companies have mentoring programs (Cronin, Nicola, 2020).
- Of those with a mentor, 97 percent say they are valuable (Cronin, Nicola, 2020).
- But only 37 percent of professionals have a mentor (Cronin, Nicola, 2020).
- 89 percent of those who have been mentored will also go on to mentor others (Cronin, Nicola, 2020).

Did you know that Steve Jobs had mentored Mark Zuckerberg in the early days of Facebook? Even more interesting is what Steve told Mark to do. "He told me that in order to reconnect with what I believed is the mission of the company, I should visit this temple that he had gone to in India early in his evolution of thinking about what he wanted Apple and his vision of the future to be," said Mark (Zuckerberg, n.d.).

This makes me wonder, "Is ego what gets in the way of success? If we took more advice like Mark did, would we achieve more?"

"It marks a big step in your development when you come to realize that other people can help you do a better job than you could do alone."

—ANDREW CARNEGIE

Another great example of both a mentor/mentee happens to be Andrew Carnegie. Andrew Carnegie is known as one of the greatest philanthropists in the world. He was born in 1835 in Scotland and came with his family to the US at the age of thirteen. His first mentor was his uncle, George Lauder Sr., who had insisted he and his cousin give speeches and perform skits. His uncle was like a father figure to him; he stated, "A man whose influence on me cannot be underestimated, my Uncle Lauder." He had started working his way up at the age of thirteen by working in a cotton mill. Then only a year later, he started working as a messenger for a local telegraph company. Here, he taught himself to use the equipment and was promoted to being a telegraph operator. It was during this time that Andrew had gained another mentor by the name of Thomas A. Scott, who had admired Andrew's efficiency and asked him to join the company where he was the superintendent at—the Pennsylvania Railroad.

This was when Andrew's income had increased as well as his connections. At the age of eighteen, Andrew had greater responsibility, but with the help of his mentor, Thomas A. Scott, was able to navigate these responsibilities and grow. One day, Andrew had a major test of his skills, which required him to make a quick and important decision while his mentor, Thomas, was away. Andrew took a calculated risk and had given orders to his workers under Thomas A. Scott's signature. His actions were able to get the situation under control. Only hours later when Thomas had arrived, a scared Andrew had to explain to him what had happened. Thomas was surprised and had walked away without saying a word. However, the next day Andrew had learned from a coworker that Thomas had been praising him for his proactive thinking and decision-making.

Andrew had learned valuable skills, so much so, he got the position of superintendent at the Pennsylvania Railroad at the age of twenty-four. He then started to make independent decisions that proved to be successful. He even came up with a technique to solve problems never used before but still had become the company's standard procedure. Andrew and his mentor Thomas were now interested in growing the company even further. They had started to build bigger coaches, freight cars as well as longer trains to carry bigger quantities and more passengers. Also, they had turned the Pennsylvania Railroad into a twenty-four-hour, seven-days-a-week telegraph and train service, which was a big accomplishment.

At a young age, Andrew had gained respect within the industry. Andrew knew the importance of learning and had taught himself many things. Even while he was self-taught in many areas, he still had guidance along the way. Being the voracious reader he was, he was given a chance to learn more by Colonel James Anderson, a retired merchant who had opened his library to "working boys," which was rare at the time. He had developed a great respect for libraries. Eventually, Andrew even helped to organize the military telegraph system during the Civil War (1861–1865) but decided to go back to working at the Pennsylvania Railroad. Regardless, with every new role, Andrew learned more.

When Andrew's father passed away, Thomas A. Scott became a father figure to him. With the help of Thomas, Andrew was able to implement a new idea in the railroad industry, which was sleeping coaches in trains. This idea had been profitable and earned Andrew a substantial increase in salary. He was then able to move his family to a new and improved home.

As a team, Andrew and Thomas were given greater responsibilities and helped each other to grow. Andrew started to invest in several small iron companies, a company that made bridges, and a manufacturer of railroad sleeping cars. As well as in oil discoveries in Pennsylvania, by investing in a small petroleum company. This is when his career began to really take off. His investments did well but instead of spending it, he grew his sights even further. He realized the potential in international business where he started to sell American railroad bonds as well as business bonds in England. He was reported to have become a millionaire from the commissions of selling these bonds. Andrew, with the approval of his mentor Thomas, was able to quit the Pennsylvania Railroad and never need to work for a paycheck again.

With a knack for innovation, Andrew then started to study the British steel industry. He had focused on learning as much as he could about the steel industry and came up with a brilliant idea to focus on growing the American steel industry. He noticed that steel would revolutionize the construction industry, so he went to his mentor Thomas to help him raise the capital he needed to be able to build his own steel plant.

This move was monumental to his career as well as the American steel industry. After Andrew's mentor Thomas died, he was able to continue to grow the steel plant. By 1900, Andrew's iron and steel company was producing more iron and steel than Great Britain's entire industry.

Andrew, with the help of his partner Charles M. Schwab, sold his business to J.P. Morgan for $480 million and then became the world's richest man. He then started to distribute his wealth to many causes. This has helped shape the world in many areas including the funding of thousands of public libraries, which made him the largest individual investor in public libraries in American history, and also funded education and international peace.

Andrew Carnegie had built an empire with the help of a few mentors and partners along the way. While we often see an individual's success, we often do not see the people who helped that individual get there. In Andrew's case, a few select mentors helped guide and grow the confidence he needed to succeed. While these mentors may not have known at the time they were mentoring the next richest man in the world, they were doing their part in helping him as a young child to grow into a more capable individual.

> *"Teamwork is the ability to work together toward a common vision. The ability to direct individual accomplishments toward organizational objectives. It is the fuel that allows common people to attain uncommon results."*
>
> —ANDREW CARNEGIE

Teachers and mentors are very important to success. Even so, only around 37 percent of people currently have one (Comaford, 2019). If more people had mentors, we would be able to achieve our goals much faster. Mentors help avoid mistakes, see opportunity, and help make more of the right decisions from their valuable experience.

If you want to get somewhere faster, find a good mentor.

The more I started reaching out to experienced leaders and asking them for advice, the more I learned. I was able to be more confident in making decisions and I had the ability to make decisions faster as well. Seeking out mentors can help you to grow at a much more rapid pace. Most people learn this lesson later in life; if they could apply this sooner, then they will excel tremendously.

> "Get around people who have something of value to share with you. Their impact will continue to have a significant effect on your life long after they have departed."
>
> —JIM ROHN

Another example of a person who became successful through having a mentor is Jim Rohn. Jim Rohn was an American entrepreneur, author, and motivational speaker. He was born on September 17, 1930, in Idaho to a farming family who taught him about hard work. Although Jim had great storytelling ability, he needed guidance. By age twenty-five, he was having a hard time financially and had to find a way to provide for his wife and child. At this time, he decided to go to an event his friend invited him to. That event changed his entire life.

At this event, Jim met an influential figure named Earl Shoaff. The meeting was instrumental for Jim's life as Earl Shoaff was the key figure in helping Jim to transform his life. For the next five years Earl Shoaff had become Jim's mentor. Earl had helped Jim to learn the fundamental principles of life such as how to work harder on himself than on his job. Personal development was the main focus.

To Jim, it was the hardest assignment of them all since personal development lasts a lifetime. Yet, he was determined to learn and was able to create one of the largest organizations in the company he had been working for. Jim had improved so much that he was selected as the vice president of the company within five years.

After five years of meeting, Earl had passed away. Before his passing, Earl had dared Jim to become a millionaire. One year later, Jim had fulfilled his mentor's wish. He was great at keeping his word.

However, the company went out of business within a few years and Jim had to look for another opportunity. He received an invitation to speak at a meeting at his Rotary Club. He accepted the invitation not knowing it would change the trajectory of his life, again. After this opportunity, Jim was asked to speak at other meetings and events., which had led to Jim hosting his first public seminar in Beverly Hills.

This is when his speaking career began and he was presenting all over the country. He continued speaking for over forty years and has impacted millions of people across the world. After having great success with his own mentor, he began mentoring others such as Tony Robbins. "That man, that seminar, that day—what Jim Rohn did was put me back in control of my own future. I took [his] message to heart and became obsessed—I would never stop growing, never stop giving, never stop trying to expand my influence or my capacity to give and do good," he stated. Jim remembered to give back what he had received. Because of this, he has helped millions of people through his books, speeches, and indirectly through the people he had mentored.

"Whatever good things we build end up building us."
—JIM ROHN

Having more than one mentor as well as teacher is best. The better you get along with each other, the easier it will be to build a productive relationship. The best mentors are the ones that make time for you. In the corporate world, the board of directors are the official "mentors" of a company. This shows how great the necessity and importance of having one or more mentors is for your life.

Eventually, you may learn so much through your mentor, that you may even become a mentor yourself. Giving back to future generations through mentorship is one of the greatest things a person can do.

"Give a man a fish, and you feed him for a day. Teach a man to fish, and you feed him for a lifetime."

—ANONYMOUS

MENTOR READINESS ASSESSMENT

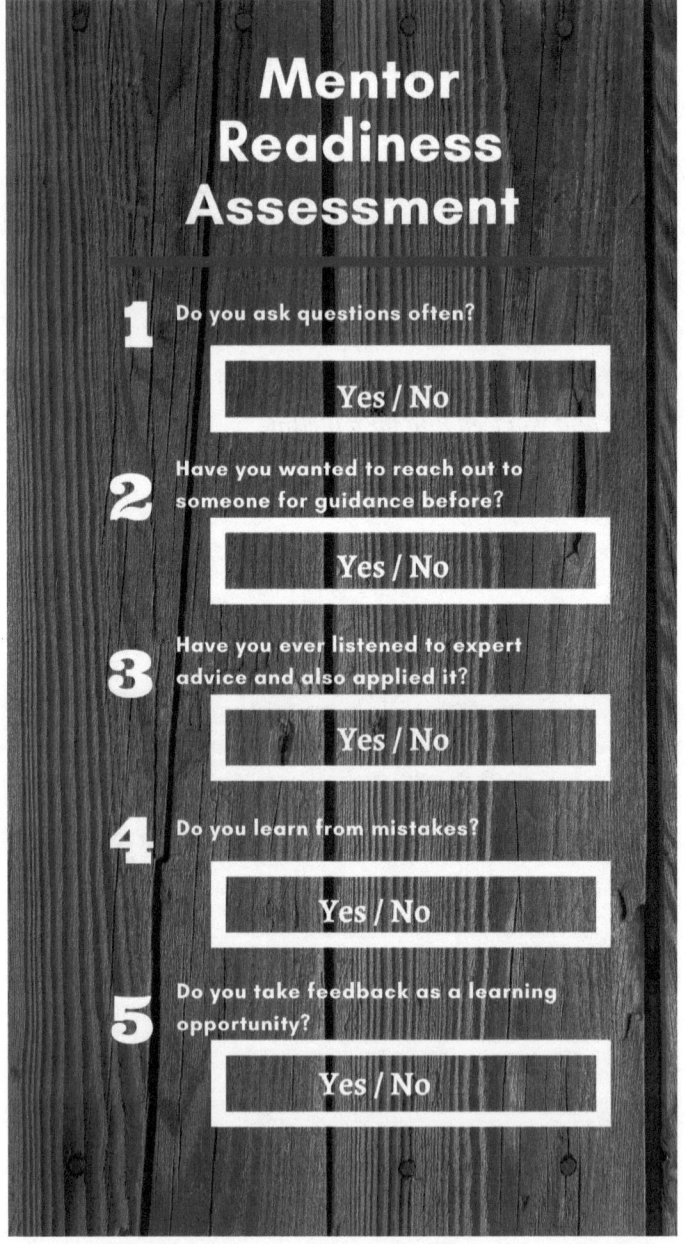

Answers:
Add up the number of times you chose "Yes."
5/5 - Good job! Not only are you ready for a mentor, but you can also possibly be one yourself!
4/5 - Great! You have the potential to have a great mentor by your side.
3/5 - Almost ready! You may want a mentor but should make sure you're ready to receive their guidance first.
2/5 - Keep going. With simple shifts, you can also be mentor-ready!
1/5 - Try again after you have implemented some of the strategies in this book!

PART 3

ACTION-TO-MOMENTUM MINDSET

CHAPTER 10

STARTING YOUR IDEA

"Ideas are responsible for the progression and prosperity of humans – without them, we would still be living in prehistoric times. No idea is too small, and all sorts of ideas have potential to change the world as we know it for the better."

—RICHARD BRANSON

"Wow!" I thought as I listened to the PETA founder and president, Ingrid Newkirk, explain her mission. At the time she was seventy years old and still going strong in the fight for animal rights. One of the most powerful women, and one of action. She told me something I had never known before—how her efforts with PETA made veganism mainstream. However, success for them was not easy. "Today, if people are young, they have no idea of course of the struggle, they just go into a store, and everything's marked vegan," she laughs. "But, in the old days, it wasn't like that; we had to work hard to even get people to go vegan for ethical reasons, environmental reasons; people laughed at that[…]no more." She has continued for decades to change laws and outdated cultural practices for the protection of our beautiful creatures and even created a company to be able to do so.

THE IDEA PUSH

Everything starts with an idea. It tends to begin with a lot of motivation but can stall with setbacks and trials. This is why it is important to have passion. Not just any passion, but a strong amount. This will help guard you in times of difficulties to push your idea forward.

A person who is a renowned illustration of this is Richard Branson. We all may know of Richard Branson and his company the Virgin Group, the parent company of over sixty of his ventures, such as Virgin Atlantic the airline company and Virgin Galactic, a newer company with a goal to provide suborbital spaceflights to tourists and also suborbital launches for space science missions. But did you know it all started with a magazine called Student, which happened to be his very first company? He had started this company in 1966 at the age of sixteen and had secured $8,000 worth of advertising for its first issue (Stephanie, 2019). He did not have to sell a single copy of the magazine; he was able to give away around fifty thousand copies of it, increasing his brand identity as well as his consumer base. Then only a few years later, he started Virgin Records which rose to monumental success over a short period of time.

In 1992, Richard was offered a staggering one billion dollars for the company. He took the offer, but instead of being happy, he was in tears. After he had told his staff he had sold the company, he went home with tears streaming on his face. "I, literally, I did have tears streaming down my face[…]. Then I ran past a sign that said, 'Branson sells for a billion.' I thought, 'I hope no photographer is going to catch me running past this sign with tears streaming down my face.' It looked very, very strange."

Why was Richard so upset? A billion dollars seems like a great deal. It was because he views a company as a group of people, which is true. At the time, Richard had to sell Virgin Records to protect his other companies from also going under. The reason being British Airways was trying to compete with him. They were even using tactics that would undermine Richard's brand with outright lies. These unethical techniques, however, did not work. What Richard did was fight back. He took British Airways to court and won. At the time, it was the largest libel settlement in UK history.

Even with all the issues that came up with running his corporation; Richard continued to grow his company. He started Virgin Airlines after his flight to the British Virgin Islands was cancelled. Being the witty entrepreneur he is, he decided to then charter a plane and charge the other travelers who had been scheduled to be on the same previous flight with him a small amount to join this new flight. Of course, most of them accepted. Realizing the potential, Richard had then researched what Boeing airliners were for sale. He found a 747 that happened to be available. This is how the idea for Virgin Airlines came into fruition.

Being known as one of the most adventurous billionaires, Richard is not one to shy away from new ideas. As much as he takes on new ideas in his professional life, he does the same personally. "Fun is one of the most important and underrated ingredients in any successful venture." This was seen when he made international news in 1987 when he tried to set a record to cross the Atlantic in a hot air balloon. He made history and successfully completed the trip. However, the balloon caught on fire at the end of his journey and started to descend momentarily from thirty thousand feet in the air. He and his copilot then jumped into the cold, shark-infested waters of the Atlantic Ocean only to be rescued by the Royal Navy, nearly two hours later! This idea did not go as planned.

"My interest in life comes from setting myself huge, apparently unachievable challenges and trying to rise above them." This has helped him to navigate the world of business as well. "Overcoming fear is the first step to success for entrepreneurs. The winners all exemplify that, and the hard work and commitment they have shown underlines what is needed to set up a business." An example is Virgin Galactic, which he created to make space flight more viable for tourists. Most may think this idea is too ambitious, but he recently completed his first space mission and became the first man to travel to space in his own rocket.

Being one of the most skilled people in the world at starting an idea and growing it to greater heights, he has not only created dozens of successful companies but has created an empire that spans multiple industries. "Virgin started with one simple idea, which developed into many new ideas, which grew in turn to foster some wider ideas in all sorts of sectors and markets. Had we not believed in our simple idea and acted upon it, we wouldn't be where we are today."
—Richard Branson

BRINGING IDEAS TO REALITY

Ideas at first are not often valued. In 1899, cars were often called the "horseless carriage" and were thought to be a luxury. It was even looked at as a fad by many of the top minds of the time. However, in 1908, the Ford Motor Company created the Model T automobile, which made up over half the automobiles in the US just ten years later. Cars had become both affordable and mainstream, baffling earlier predictions. This teaches us that we can't look to others, even experts, to know whether an idea will work or not. It is up to us to try, even if it is uncertain.

When I first heard of Tesla many years ago, I had no clue what it was. Let alone who it was named after. Now everyone knows of Tesla. Did you know it was named after a famous inventor born in 1856? He created things so far-fetched that it would have changed the world as we know it today. However, competing companies had sabotaged his well-meaning inventions. Luckily, Elon Musk came along and continued Tesla's work. Even buying out the name Tesla for his new company. Because Tesla had created his many inventions decades ago, he was able to lay the groundbreaking work that was needed for future generations to complete.

Fun fact: Elon Musk became the richest man on the same day Tesla had died seventy-eight years before, on January seventh!

"Everything is a calculated risk. You have to take action."
—ROBERT ANGEL

When I spoke with Robert Angel, I knew it was going to be an interesting conversation. He is an author, inventor, speaker, and self-confessed explorer. He happens to be the creator behind the international best-selling board game Pictionary, which you may have played with. As a child, Robert knew he wanted to be an entrepreneur when he grew up. He also definitely didn't want to work for anyone else and was open to whatever opportunity would come.

Out of the blue, Robert came across the idea for Pictionary in 1982 after college while living with his three roommates. However, he didn't start Pictionary until three years later while only using a few simple tools like the Webster's dictionary, a No. 2 pencil, and a yellow legal pad. As he played the game with his roommates, he would notice they had so much fun. He didn't think of it as just a game; he thought of it as a positive, emotional experience. He wanted to share this feeling with the world. Although he had no plan or dream, Robert started creating the game and put his first thousand games together, by hand, in a tiny apartment.

The inventing process was challenging for Robert but was also fun. He embraced the process and loved it. He also loved the challenge of being able to bring the game to life. No manual was available to him at the time on how to produce, sell, and market a game, so Robert and his partners had made their own. They had used their intuition to move forward.

As he designed the game and was putting it together, he was doing it in his apartment. He and his partners had nine different companies supplying them with parts for his game. The last part that he needed to be done was the collating of the cards, which means to collect and combine in the proper order. They had already sent out their invitations to have their launch. There were nine days before the launch; they couldn't cancel it, but their printer said he couldn't get the cards collating. His task was to sort half a million game cards because they had one thousand games and five hundred cards per game. He was going to give them stacks of five hundred per game, but he couldn't. Now, Robert and his team were scrambling and panic-stricken since they had about seven days to fix the issue. That was their mission.

They had to figure out how to collate and sort the cards fast. They went to Nordstrom and retrieved 170 shoe boxes and moved all of Robert's furniture out of his apartment into his bedroom, put up five eight-foot folding rented tables, and placed them in the apartment in a maze formation, and the shoe boxes around it, and literally started hand sorting them one by one. There were three of them and if they weren't working at their jobs, they were collating the cards every minute of every day. They finally got it completed in six days, working sixteen hours a day. Within one hour before the launch, they had put them in the boxes and completed the task.

This had been the first major test of their resolve. On the outside, it seemed terrible, but it had turned out to be good for Robert and his team. He says it didn't happen to them; it happened for them because they wound up getting over the massive challenge together. They knew they had each other's backs and now had gotten to know each other better. They really bonded over the terrible moment, which to Robert was like the common enemy. They had risen to the challenge together. At the start, it wasn't comfortable, but in the end it was the best thing that ever happened to them as a team. It ended up setting up their partnership for the next fifteen years. Starting an idea can help you form lifelong bonds in the process.

The game was a massive hit. They needed to scale the business, but they just didn't have the financing and they couldn't go to a venture capitalist because it just wasn't happening at that time. So, to get the game into as many hands as possible, they had to license the game to another company that would do the manufacturing, distribution, marketing, and sales, and pay them a royalty. Milton Bradley, the biggest game company in the world, offered to do this. Robert had done a lot of work to get to this point, only fourteen months after they had launched it.

Robert was twenty-six years old when looking at this contract. To him, it was a good contract. It was the biggest royalty they had ever given a company. They had given them everything they wanted and all he had to do was sign the contract so he was on a beach in Florida. He would have his new car and could retire. He had worked for this moment. Yet three things had to happen for him to sign the contract and finally get to the beach.

One, the company had to have brand integrity; they had to respect Pictionary's brand integrity, which meant the rules, the graphics, the game play because that was what Pictionary was. Second, they had to have the resources to get it done because if they were going to take it big, they had to be able to do it well. Luckily, they could do that. The intangible one for them was their values. Their corporate values had to align. They had to think like Robert and his team did and they had to be good citizens. Everyone was saying, "Rob, you got to sign the contract! Go!" However, they couldn't trust them because they had come to them earlier and wanted to change the packaging. Regardless of Robert and his team saying no, they couldn't trust the company to not change the packaging because they wouldn't put that in the contract.

This became a trust issue. Not a money issue, not a resource issue. Can they trust them with no plan B and nowhere to go? With no backup, they said no. Robert was willing and prepared to go back to waiting tables, rather than signing a deal that didn't make sense. Also, his intuition had told him not to. It was screaming at him, "Don't sign this deal."

Robert had stuck to his intuition, and he didn't sign the deal.

The very next day when he was in his warehouse at 7 a.m., packing boxes to ship, he starts to think, "What have I done?" Two months later, while he is still selling and marketing, another company comes to them with everything that they wanted! An even bigger royalty rate, packaging agreement, and all the guarantees. If they had said yes to the deal that didn't feel right, they wouldn't have gotten the deal that was right. One of the biggest reasons that Pictionary is successful as well as Robert is because of the moments he does indeed listen to his intuition. "It's that moment where your gut, your heart overrides what your brain is telling you. My brain told me to sign that contract, but my intuition said no." In Robert's case, it had turned out well to stay true to the idea he started.

During Robert and his team's journey, we can see that challenges were constant. With focus, determination, and holding on to their shared vision, they succeeded in not only creating a beloved game but a company that was the biggest selling game in the world at one point. It has spanned sixty countries and sold thirty-eight million games until they sold it to Mattel in 2001.

Both Richard Branson and Robert Angel implemented their ideas immediately after they came up with them. After overcoming many trials, they were able to successfully grow them. You may have even been a customer of their products and services. When starting your idea, you do not need to know everything. You just have to start.

TOOLS TO USE
When starting an idea, you will need tools. What tools? The most important tools are knowledge and persistence. The tools you cannot see are the most needed. Starting an idea takes the best plan of action and accounts for how the market is doing, your financial capability, and also navigates the legal aspects of a business. However, a business can thrive even if you only know about one of these aspects; you can learn the rest as you go. As most do.

During the pandemic, an entrepreneur I know was able to do well with his company, Secret Knock, which is rated as the number one networking event in the world. As a luxury brand and event company you would think it would have had to be put on pause, but through his networking skills he was able to sell out his events. As well as have fun while doing it.

He used his knowledge and persistence to get through the hurdles that had come up.

Tools you need when starting an idea can be the very same tools you need when unexpected changes occur when you are already in the market.

CHAPTER 11

HOW TO DEVELOP AN ACTION-TO-MOMENTUM MINDSET

"Momentum solves 80 percent of your problems."
—JOHN C. MAXWELL

"People who succeed have momentum. The more they succeed, the more they want to succeed, and the more they find a way to succeed."
—TONY ROBBINS

WILLPOWER

If anyone can be an example of an action-to-momentum mindset, it is Lori Greiner. Her take on this is "a brilliant idea doesn't guarantee a successful invention. Real magic comes from a brilliant idea combined with willpower, tenacity, and a willingness to make mistakes" (Roysam, 2016).

You see, Lori Greiner started her career with one product, but she was able to then go on to create over five hundred products, as well as have over 120 US and international patents (Lori, n.d.). Known as the "Queen of QVC," she is also a Shark on the hit television show *Shark Tank*, and has been for over a decade. She is known for having the ability to tell instantly if a product is a "hero or a zero" (Lori, n.d.). She also has a mind-blowing 90 percent success rate on new items she has launched.

Lori Greiner did not come from an inventing background; she was born in Chicago and her mother was a psychologist and her father was a real estate developer (Parker, n.d.). She was taught at a young age by her parents to earn a living from her own business rather than be an employee (Parker, n.d). Her first product, however, was borne out of necessity. She had never planned to be an inventor, but she had a great idea and ran with it.

It all started in 1996, when Lori chatted about earrings with her friend and about how she thought jewelry boxes were a "nightmare." At the time, she had quite the collection of jewelry and had been making and selling her own jewelry (Roysam, 2016). Then, all of a sudden, she had a brilliant idea. "It was a thunderbolt moment. It just—bam!—hit me."

Her idea was an innovative earring organizer that was plastic with sliding shelves that could hold over a hundred pairs of earrings. It sounds like a simple idea, but in the mid-nineties it was a revolutionary product. Her first steps were to look for Chicago-based manufacturers that could help her mold her new product. She also did what many new entrepreneurs don't do: get consumer feedback. She asked women she did not know what they thought of the homemade wood model of her product. She knew with the feedback she received, she had a winning product. "I felt certain that an earring organizer, like my concept, was something everyone would love because everyone needed it. It was completely different than anything that had ever been offered and it was a much better solution." She then quickly took her next steps, which highlights her action-oriented mindset.

At the age of twenty-eight, Lori had gotten a $300,000 loan to further build her product. She was then able to start the production of her first earring holder only a month after having the idea. After her product was manufactured, she pursued the retailer JCPenney to carry it. "I would call just a thousand times. I would call again and again until I just got lucky, and they happened to pick up the phone." The buyer who answered her call challenged Lori to sell her product to all of the fourteen JCPenney stores in the Chicago area at the time (Robehmed, 2012). Not only was Lori able to persuade the then giant retailer, but she was able to land a deal that allowed her to invent products for them.

> *"Know your product or business idea and show it quickly."*
>
> —LORI GREINER

In the same year Lori landed the deal, she started her very first company, For Your Ease Only Inc. Lori's next steps were to sell her product on television. She was able to make an appearance on the *Home Shopping Network* and had sold out of two thousand pieces in only five minutes, which then prompted her expansion into more products (Robehmed, 2012). "With the success of each thing, I kept thinking of more and more."

In eighteen months, Lori was able to pay off her loan of $300,000. Her success didn't stop there; she started her own show on QVC in 2000 called *Clever and Unique Creations*, which became one of the longest-running shows on the network.

After her initial success, Lori had picked up speed. "In the beginning, I was just thinking as fast as I could to come up with more and more. I'd look for problems that people experience in everyday life. Then I would think about how an item could come to life" (Hochwald, 2017). Then in 2012, Lori landed the biggest opportunity yet.

She was given the chance to be a panelist on *Shark Tank*, a critically acclaimed and multi-Emmy-Award-winning entrepreneurial-themed reality show. She was called by the casting director, who said, "You're a unicorn[…]. America could learn a lot from you" (Hochwald, 2017). Quite the compliment, as a unicorn is a term for a privately held company with over a billion-dollar valuation. Lori was immediately on board.

Lori's notoriety and reach were now growing at a monumental speed. "In business, it is most often all about getting your foot in the door and once you do, everything opens up and things start to naturally progress into bigger and more opportunities." Even while competing with several other successful entrepreneurs on the show for business deals, she has the ability to hold her own and has become well-known for her impeccable negotiating skills and her uncanny ability to know and identify emerging brands and invest in them (CNBC, n.d.).

Her action-to-momentum mindset has continued to keep opportunities coming her way. Even years later, many of her investments are some of the most successful stories on *Shark Tank*, such as Scrub Daddy, a kitchen-sponge line with $209 million in sales as well as Simply Fit Board, a balance-board workout tool with $160 million in lifetime sales. She also has a stake in ten of the top twenty companies.

In terms of investing, Lori sees beyond the product. "I prefer to like the people I invest in, but it's not an absolute necessity, as long as they have a good mind and I know they'll do whatever it takes to be successful." She is a person who genuinely likes to help people. She never set out to be a millionaire, "My driving force comes out of a creative need. I love creating products and sharing them with others." This is one of the many reasons she is known as "the Warm-Blooded Shark" (Lori, n.d.).

Lori Greiner has developed quite an effective action-to-momentum mindset throughout her career. One of the ways she was able to do so was that she was hands on during the process of growing her career. By validating that there actually was an interest in her product before she had ever taken action in its creation, she was able to build the momentum she needed for it to take off. Once it took off, she kept the momentum going while learning many lessons along the way.

"In the beginning I was really, really lean. For the longest time I did it all. I played every hat. I was in the factory, doing the graphic design, the photography, the selling—literally everything. I saved money doing what I could myself. It was hard but I learned. I learned that nobody's better than you to get your business off the ground. The experience you get is priceless" (Yahoo!, n.d.).

Lori's search for solutions has created the momentum needed to build the products that people want and has helped her to develop an action-to-momentum mindset. Not only did she start creating an idea without having the experience and resources she needed, but she also made sure to keep the momentum going once she did have a successful product of her own. We can see that solving problems is the best way to create an action-to-momentum mindset.

"As an entrepreneur, you can always find a solution if you try hard enough."

—LORI GREINER

RELENTLESS

"A dream written down with a date becomes a goal. A goal broken down into steps becomes a plan. A plan backed by action makes your dreams come true."

—GREG REID

Greg Reid is a man of many talents and is always willing to help. Having a way with words, count on him to give you encouragement when you need it. I am always surprised at the enthusiasm he has when he speaks. He is a best-selling author, keynote speaker, entrepreneur, and movie producer. He grew up in sunny San Diego, known to be the hidden gem of California and also considered to be "America's Finest City" (About San Diego, n.d.). This is where Greg started his successful advertising company and sold it for a considerable amount, launching him into the influential and motivational advisor he is today. The secret to his success? Tapping into the successful actions of others.

An important principle Greg follows to this day is to listen to the advice of people who have already done what it is he wants to do. When he went to climb Mount Kilimanjaro, he didn't ask a tourist how to climb it; he asked a Sherpa who had climbed it many times before. The advice he continually lives by is "*Seek council, not opinion.*" When you seek council, not opinion, you have a greater chance to succeed because you are getting advice from people who have already done what you are trying to do and know how to do it.

A good example of seeking council is when Greg released a best-selling book. It had received many great reviews, but one person had given it a negative review. This had upset him, so he reached out to a friend of his who gave him the keen advice to "illuminate" it. Greg took his friend's advice and sent an email to thirty-seven thousand people and told them, "Hey everyone, my book's out. People seem to love it; one guy says it sucks." Then he linked the review to his audience, and this resulted in his book becoming a best seller again because of all their support. You see, Greg didn't wait to see what would happen; he had made sure to get the advice he needed and then took action to get the results he wanted.

Astonishingly, Greg received a letter of recommendation from the Napoleon Hill Foundation and was hand selected to help carry on the teaching found in their book, *Think and Grow Rich*, regarded as the best-selling self-help book of all time. (Think and Grow Rich, n.d.). This honor gave him the access to meet almost anyone he wanted to in the world, including Steve Wozniak the cofounder of Apple and Frank Shankwitz, the founder of the Make-A-Wish Foundation. As a result, Greg has authored the book *Three Feet from Gold: Turn Your Obstacles into Opportunities; A Think and Grow Rich Series* with them.

Having a gift for communication, Greg has now also become a Forbes, Inc. and Entrepreneur top ten rated keynote speaker (Conner, 2016), as well has been given an honor by the White House and former President Bill Clinton for his work on mentoring youth in his hometown of San Diego.

Greg also spent six considerable years making a film he produced for Frank Shankwitz, the founder of the Make-A-Wish Foundation, which is known for granting children all over the world more than five hundred thousand wishes spanning over forty years. The origin for this film came to be during a conversation Greg had with Frank. He asked Frank, *"What is your wish? I'll grant you your wish?"* Frank's response, *"No one has ever asked…I just want my story to be told so my grandkids know I did something."* As of now, the film has trended worldwide on Netflix and has made the final list for the Oscars. Greg has enabled the legacy of Frank Shankwitz to continue and help many with the film despite Frank's passing in early 2021.

Greg's relentless actions have helped countless others with wisdom and advice. He has been published in over one hundred books including thirty-two best sellers in over forty-five languages. Being true to his motto of *"All I want in life, is to give life my all,"* he continues to inspire many with his deeds, resulting in him receiving two honorary PhDs as well as a star on the Las Vegas Walk of Stars. We can see with the example of his life, that taking massive action leads to powerful results.

We also can see that before Greg takes action, he listens to the wisdom of others who have successfully completed the task at hand. This way he is able to create the momentum needed to accomplish his goals in a much easier way. He is able to learn what he should avoid and what strategies he should use through the experience of others.

When we see the results of other's work, we often think it came suddenly. What we don't see is the many years of hard work spent accumulating the skills and talents to get them to where they are today. The very skills that helped them to develop momentum. Like an artist, it can take years of practice to become skilled at a craft, yet they don't count the years as they go by waiting for the final day that they can achieve master status. The act of art tends to be an enjoyable endeavor and they immerse themselves in it. This is how we should be in whatever undertaking we do. We should immerse ourselves into what we do to achieve the results that we want.

Developing an action-to-momentum mindset is important. Even when we can't see the finish line, it is important to take incremental steps toward our goals. It is in this progress we can eventually see the results we seek.

IMMERSION

When I immerse myself into a project that I am passionate about, I don't think about much else in that moment. This is what is so important about listening to our own intuition when it comes to our future. I have found that when I make the decision to follow my passion, it is also important to take action since it gives me the momentum that I need to get to where I want to go. Isn't it great that momentum accumulates? If Steve Jobs had not taken the calligraphy classes he did in college, he would not have had the inspiration to have created Apple's beautiful typography that we use now. He stated, "When I was attending the calligraphy classes at college, I could never imagine that skill or learning will have any practical application in my life. But ten years later, when we were designing the first Macintosh computer, it all came back to me. And we designed all my learning into the Mac. Had I never dropped in on that calligraphy course

in college, the Mac would have never had multiple typefaces or beautifully proportionate font styles."

I once heard of the phrase, "Evolve or go extinct." This resonated with me because it is true. I believe we need to evolve and continue to better ourselves in a rapidly changing world. It is always changing and accepting this will help us to adapt better. In the future our technology will help us to communicate even better than we do now, travel faster, and advance us in ways that we never knew could exist. If we anticipate this now, we can hit the ground running when this takes place and have an action plan ready to go. If our mindset is primed, successful actions will follow.

ACTION PLAN

Research shows that having an action plan is important in preventing anger from disrupting your goals (Dolan, 2019). Action planning functions as a guide for people and may aid them in keeping their attention and motivation focused on on-task behaviors and not getting distracted by their feelings of anger. When people experience anger during goal pursuit and have generated a strong action plan, this might help them to direct their motivational resources toward focusing on future aspects, thus directing behavior toward key activities in the goal achievement process (Schmitt, 2019).

It is easy to become distracted by anger; however, focusing on your next task can shorten or even eliminate this emotion. Action planning helps with overcoming what we feel now so we can focus on better things to come.

KEY POINTS

Here are quick ways to develop an action plan to get the momentum you want. Surprisingly, many do not take advantage of these activities.

1. A calendar
2. To do list
3. Removing distractions
4. Having deadlines
5. Holding yourself accountable

These are the easiest ways to start. Now all you need to do is find the strategy that works for you. Once you have planned your action steps, you will need to start making moves to build the momentum needed for continued success.

Developing an action-to-momentum mindset takes practice. We can see through both Lori and Greg's journeys that developing an action-to-momentum mindset can impact every area in your life. They continue to use this approach in their daily lives, which serves them well.

Action helps build the momentum needed to achieve success. Momentum can also be described as progress. No matter how small, progress is important. "Progress equals happiness," according to Tony Robbins. Once you overcome your own fears and use your mindset for you instead of against you, you will start to get more results. We may not be able to connect all the dots of all our actions taken today, but in the future they will start to make a little more sense. It is in the process that we start to find out what we are really made of.

CHAPTER 12

AMBITIOUS APTITUDE

"Take a chance! All life is a chance. The man who goes farthest is generally the one who is willing to do and dare."

—DALE CARNEGIE

Ambitious aptitude is the ability to achieve success through determination. Ambition, when used in the right way, can be a positive quality. When we can achieve success for ourselves, we are then able to help others achieve that same success.

One notable ambitious person who has inspired many is Dale Carnegie. Dale Carnegie has impacted millions of individuals throughout the years with his teachings on self-improvement. Most notably through his book *How to Win Friends and Influence People*. This book was first published in 1936 and still remains a best seller, having sold over fifteen million books worldwide. Dale's teachings are as relevant now as they were when they were first taught; wisdom stands the test of time.

Dale did not start out with a silver spoon in his mouth. He had ambitions and went after them at a time where it was harder to be able to do so. He was born on November 24, 1888, in Missouri on a farm. As a young boy he had to milk cows everyday early in the morning at 4 a.m. before school. As a teen, he realized he enjoyed public speaking and joined the debate team in high school. Little did he know this was the beginning of a long and fruitful career.

However, when he tried to join the debate team in college, it didn't work out. He didn't have the right apparel to be accepted by the students there since he was not as wealthy as they were. Also, he had to ride to and from school every day on horseback. As hard as this was, he made sure to practice reciting speeches and his oratory style, refusing to give up. He had steadfast ambition. After watching a speaker, copying their speaking style as well as mannerisms, Dale became a hit—so much so that he started to give speaking lessons at his school.

This helped him well when he started his career as a salesman. He became the most successful salesman in Omaha making his sales territory the national leader of the company. His ambition drove him to learn a new talent, so he enrolled in the American Academy of Dramatic Arts in New York City. He became an actor for a short time, until he realized he wanted to use his speaking skills to build a career instead. This was more possible now because there were more opportunities for speakers in New York than there were in his hometown.

Dale began his career by teaching public speaking classes at a YMCA after persuading the manager (Biography, 2014). His classes started taking off and were received well. He then expanded his classes to more YMCAs in additional major cities. After fine-tuning his techniques, he started to develop his own approach.

Dale became so good he started to write books on public speaking. As his ambitions grew, so did his actions. The very next year, Dale changed the spelling of his last name to "Carnegie" to match that of successful businessman Andrew Carnegie. This happened after Dale had spoken to a sold-out crowd at the Carnegie Hall in New York City, one of the buildings Andrew Carnegie funded through his philanthropy.

Changing your last name was very uncommon then, but Dale was willing to do things most others were not. He would even observe international public speakers to get insight on how to improve his craft. One such insight was that most enthusiastic speakers drew the largest audiences, so he then made enthusiasm a key part of his philosophy and incorporated it into his popular "Dale Carnegie Course." Corporations started to send employees to take his courses, including General Motors and IBM, to train them to be more confident and successful individuals.

In a few short years, Dale had started to become more successful. However, unexpectedly, he lost all his savings in the stock market crash of 1929. He knew he had to get through this. Which he did by creating the most popular work he had ever done. The book, *How to Win Friends and Influence People*, became an international best seller and heightened his status. After years of research, including reading hundreds of biographies to learn how the world's greatest leaders achieved their success, he finally reached the success he was seeking in a field he loved.

He continued to create the Dale Carnegie Institute, which during his lifetime expanded into 750 American cities and fifteen foreign countries. His courses continue to be taught worldwide. If it were not for his ambitious aptitude, we would not have had the gift of Dale's teachings today. He has been able to help millions of people to be able to develop more confidence and business success through communication than almost any other person in history.

> *"Are you bored with life? Then throw yourself into some work you believe in with all your heart, live for it, die for it, and you will find happiness that you had thought could never be yours."*
>
> —DALE CARNEGIE

Studies show that the most ambitious cities are actually the happiest. Research has found that London, the most ambitious city on the index with a score of 404/500, scored highly on the happiness index with 7.65/10 as well (Dojo, 2021). The countries with lower scores on the ambitious index had lower levels of happiness.

The same results are true for people on an individual scale. A study done at the University of California-Riverside compared people who set ambitious goals to those who set more conservative goals. The researchers who conducted the study discovered that people who had set ambitious goals experienced greater satisfaction overall, even if they had similar outcomes to those who set conservative goals (Massan, 2021).

> "If you can dream it, you can do it."
>
> —WALT DISNEY

Many ambitious people are often very determined as well. They do not give up easily and are able to achieve huge goals regardless of it taking them many years. They persisted when the people in their lives had tried to dissuade them. Our ambitions should not be dictated by others even if they mean well. This is why we should surround ourselves with equally ambitious people so that we may have more supportive influence in our lives.

A study that was published in *Psychological Science* in 2013 found that when people are running low on self-control, they often seek out self-disciplined people to help them boost their willpower. Since self-control is important to reaching long-term goals, making friends with people who have willpower could be a secret to success (Morin, 2015).

ACCOMPLISHMENT PROCESS

"Most people are fast to stop you before you get started but hesitate to get in the way if you're moving."

—TIM FERRISS

> "It is possible to become world-class, enter the top 5 percent of performers in the world, in almost any subject within six to twelve months, or even six to twelve weeks."
> —TIM FERRISS

Another illustration of high ambition is Tim Ferriss. Tim Ferriss is an entrepreneur who was named *Fast Company*'s "Most Innovative Business People" and is one of *Fortune*'s "40 under 40." He is also an investor and author of four number one New York Times and Wall Street Journal best sellers, which include: *The 4-Hour Workweek*, *Tools of Titans*, and *Tribe of Mentors: Short Life Advice from the Best in the World*.

The 4-Hour Workweek happens to be a favorite book of mine, so it's interesting to know that Tim did not expect it to be a best seller when he wrote it; it was a surprise.

Tim was born on July 20, 1977, in East Hampton, New York. Being small for his age growing up, he would get picked on, so his mother signed him up for wrestling classes. This made him stronger and more confident. He had periods of depression in his early years and in 1999 while in college, was emotionally depleted. Luckily, his mother helped encourage him into a more positive mindset.

Tim took a year off and started to teach Japanese and worked different jobs in China; he developed a passion for different cultures during this time also. He then returned to finish his degree in East Asian Studies at Princeton. While in college, he started a few entrepreneurial ideas; none of these ideas took off. However, he was still learning about new things.

After Tim graduated, he got a sales position at a data storage company. He also began developing an online nutritional supplement business that claimed an increase in short-term memory and reaction speed effective within sixty minutes. He concentrated on selling his products to athletes. "Brain-Quicken was a real learning on-the-job MBA," he stated. This new change increased his profits, but he found himself working fourteen-hour days.

Tim was stressed and tired from his long work hours. He then started to use productive strategies to gain back more time in his life. He started to automate and outsource tasks in his business. This helped him to find time for growing his business, and he created a system that allowed him to thrive. After having more time to do the things he actually wanted to do, he booked a fifteen-month adventure. He traveled the world and came back home to a growing business. He then started to write about his discovery, which resulted in him writing *The 4-Hour Workweek*.

The 4-Hour Workweek was rejected by twenty-seven publishers before Random House finally accepted his work. They released twelve thousand copies in 2007 through their Crown imprint. It took off and spent more than four years on *The New York Times Best Seller List*, was translated into forty languages, and sold more than 2.1 million copies worldwide. He went on to become the go-to expert in multiple fields.

We may see ambition as a selfish quality; however, it is only selfish if not used for the right intentions. Tim, with his platform, has not only helped thousands of people to become better individuals through self-development and lifestyle techniques, but he has also donated millions of dollars into research.

"Success can usually be measured by the number of uncomfortable conversations we are willing to have, and by the number of uncomfortable actions, we are willing to take."

—TIM FERRISS

An ambitious aptitude can be the reason you create a successful company or pivot to a new career that turns out better than you had expected. It can help give you the push you need to start doing things on a whole new level. When you take on an ambitious aptitude, you are giving yourself the capacity to think bigger.

When I decide to take risks, it is because of having an ambitious aptitude. Most people, however, need more of a push to develop an ambitious aptitude. This is where coaches and motivational speakers can come in. There are many times in life where it is difficult to be ambitious and people tend to tread with caution. However, with almost all experience, you learn and grow. This prepares us for additional opportunities that come your way.

Oftentimes, we see the results of success without all the "behind-the-scenes" work it takes. When building an ambitious aptitude, we will need to have the key qualities of persistence, discipline, dedication, and the ability to do hard work as well as the ability to overcome disappointment. However, when you become accustomed to doing this, you will start to succeed even faster than before. The first million dollars is always the hardest to make, but after making this milestone, it tends to become easier.

SELF-ASSURED

Being ambitious does not mean being selfish. In fact, the most ambitious people can be very generous as well. Now, more than ever before, women who have ambitions typically common for men are being embraced. Having ambitions allows us to have the confidence to make the choices that both inspire us and help us to achieve our full potential. History is full of those who had great ambitions, which still impact us today. Even kids. Some of the most interesting inventions came from them, such as:

-Christmas lights
-Earmuffs
-Snowmobiles

So, when you think that you need more "experience" before you take action on your ambitions, think about these inventions which were made by kids many decades ago.

Now, because of their self-assurance to create something great, even though they were kids, we are all able to enjoy having these luxuries.

When we have ambitions, we are self-assured. Self-assurance means confidence in one's own abilities or character.

When we embrace this, we can create new paths to explore.

EPILOGUE

While on your new quest to *Take Massive Action*, take care of yourself and enjoy the journey! The most important thing you can do during this process of taking massive action is to make sure you are doing well both physically and mentally. One of the most prolific examples of this is billionaire Mark Cuban.

> "Today is the youngest you will ever be. Live like it."
> —MARK CUBAN

When I interviewed him before, he was the fastest interview turnaround I have ever completed. As busy as he is, he still continues to build momentum long after he has amassed success. His ways to take care of himself are quite simple. Maybe they may work for you as well. By shooting hoops, doing hour-long cardio routines six days a week, and occasionally taking Latin-fusion aerobic classes, he has been able to stay fit. Additionally, by turning off his phone at night he is able to take care of his mental health. What's great is you can have your own ways to care for yourself.

Create a go-to plan that helps you destress when things get overwhelming—one that you will actually do and is healthy. When you have a go-to plan that helps you destress and relax, you will have more of the physical and mental capacity to keep building the momentum you seek.

As you get used to getting out of your comfort zone, be prepared to feel a little uncomfortable and know this is okay. Rockets need pressure to launch, so don't worry if you don't feel ready in the beginning to take the first steps; what matters is that you do since it is important to *Take Massive Action* as soon as possible. Years from now, you will have made traction and may even have completed many of your dreams.

Congratulations!

As we look back at what we have learned from this book and all the people who were brave enough to *Take Massive Action*, we see one thing in common, and that is: starting. They took action and focused on what went right and pivoted when things went wrong. This is how they were able to create momentum and accomplish many goals.

Now, it's your turn.

Think about a major goal. What is it? Envision it. What are the key steps you can do now to achieve this goal later?

1.
2.
3.

"If you go to work on your goals, your goals will go to work on you. If you go to work on your plan, your plan will go to work on you. Whatever good things we build end up building us."
—JIM ROHN

LIST FIVE MORE GOALS YOU WANT TO CONQUER BELOW:

When I started to implement this principle in my own life, I started unlocking hidden talents within myself. Ones that needed to be brought into the open.

It is easy to overthink things or try to fit into the prevailing culture. This, I have learned, can get in the way of reaching goals. When I started to take steps toward my goals…

That is when the pieces of the puzzle started to fit.

ACKNOWLEDGMENTS

I would like to thank everyone who has helped put this book together.

Thank you, Eric Koester, for being the guide in this entire process and helping me get this message out.

Steve Barnett, your efforts for not only the entrepreneurial community but the world at large are amazing! Thank you for making the contributions you have. Also, I am thankful for your part in putting on the Startup Weekend powered by Google for Entrepreneurs, as it has been a huge milestone for me. Thank you!

Dr. Greg S. Reid, you are awesome. Thank you for being such a helpful contributor to this book. Your insights are profound. Also, thank you for your quick responses whenever I reach out for advice! I am always amazed by your intellect.

Martin Cooper, thank you for your insights and contributions to the world. I enjoyed learning from you.

Shawn Flynn, I am so glad we worked together on this. Thank you for your contributions.

Stephen Key, thank you for your conversation and insights. Your knowledge is a great resource to many.

Also, thank you to Mariah Bailey, Calvin Pak, Joseph Learthur Flagg Jr., and David Ridgway!

Many thanks to my editors and your tireless work.

APPENDIX

INTRODUCTION

"Action Quotes." BrainyQuote. Xplore. Accessed August 23, 2021. https://www.brainyquote.com/topics/action-quotes.

Kelly, Jack. "More than Half of US Workers Are Unhappy in Their JOBS: Here's Why and What Needs to Be Done Now." Forbes. Forbes Magazine, October 25, 2019. https://www.forbes.com/sites/jackkelly/2019/10/25/more-than-half-of-us-workers-are-unhappy-in-their-jobs-heres-why-and-what-needs-to-be-done-now/?sh=73fab8b72024.

CHAPTER 1

Carriere, B. "Mysigep." Sigma Phi Epsilon, June 14, 2018. https://sigep.org/sigepjournal/square-co-founder-jim-mckelvey-wont-quit/.

Clifford, Catherine. "Elon Musk on Working 120 Hours in a Week: 'However Hard It Was for [the Team], I Would Make It Worse for Me.'" CNBC. CNBC, December 10, 2018. https://www.cnbc.com/2018/12/10/elon-musk-says-working-120-hours-in-a-week-was-a-show-of-leadership.html

Economy, Peter. "These 11 Elon Musk Quotes Will Inspire Your Success and Happiness." Inc.com. Inc., October 24, 2017. https://www.inc.com/peter-economy/11-elon-musk-quotes-that-will-push-you-to-achieve-impossible.html.

Economy, Peter. "Tony Robbins: 19 INSPIRING POWER Quotes for Success." Inc.com. Inc., March 26, 2015. https://www.inc.com/peter-economy/tony-robbins-19-inspiring-power-quotes-for-success.html.

Fenske, Sarah. "Square's Jim Mckelvey Explains How to Build a Business, 'ONE Crazy Idea at a Time'." St. Louis Public Radio, March 27, 2020. https://news.stlpublicradio.org/show/st-louis-on-the-air/2020-03-27/squares-jim-mckelvey-explains-how-to-build-a-business-one-crazy-idea-at-a-time.

Gravier, Elizabeth. "Elon Musk Says Playing Video Games Is How He and 'Many of the Best Software Engineers' Got into Programming." CNBC. CNBC, September 4, 2020. https://www.cnbc.com/2019/06/28/elon-musk-talks-about-how-video-games-got-him-hooked-on-programming.html.

"Jim McKelvey." Forbes. Forbes Magazine. Accessed August 26, 2021. https://www.forbes.com/profile/jim-mckelvey/?sh=40006136644a.

Mann, Mark. "The Story of Elon Musk's First Company." Site Builder Report, May 5, 2021. https://www.sitebuilderreport.com/origin-stories/elon-musk#:~:text=Elon%20Musk%20might%20be%20the,only%2027%2Dyears%2Dold.

Mejia, Zameena. "Elon Musk Lived on $1 a Day When He Moved to Canada as a Teen and Other Surprising Facts About His Youth." CNBC. CNBC, December 20, 2018. https://www.cnbc.com/2018/12/20/teslas--elon-musk-9-surprising-facts-about-his-youth.html.

Meyerowitz, Robert. "Jim McKelvey Has Altered the Way Money Changes Hands. Now What?" St. Louis Magazine, March 7,

2011. https://www.stlmag.com/Jim-McKelvey-Has-Altered-the-Way-Money-Changes-Hands-Now-What/.

Somerville, Heather. "Elon Musk Moves to Texas, Takes Jab at Silicon Valley." The Wall Street Journal. Dow Jones & Company, December 9, 2020. https://www.wsj.com/articles/elon-musk-to-discuss-teslas-banner-year-despite-pandemic-silicon-valleys-future-11607449988.

SpaceX. Accessed August 25, 2021. https://www.spacex.com/mission/.

CHAPTER 2

Elkins, Kathleen. "Barbara Corcoran Worked 22 Jobs by AGE 23-Here's the One She Learned Most From." Yahoo! News. Yahoo!, March 26, 2018. https://www.yahoo.com/news/barbara-corcoran-worked-22-jobs-134100501.html.

Gallo, Carmine. "Bill Gates SAYS Steve Jobs 'Cast SPELLS' on His Audience During Presentations. Here Are 3 Ways the APPLE Wizard Worked His Magic." Inc.com. Inc., July 10, 2019. https://www.inc.com/carmine-gallo/bill-gates-says-steve-jobs-cast-spells-on-his-audience-during-presentations-here-are-3-ways-apple-wizard-worked-his-magic.html.

Greenfield, Rebecca. "The Crazy Perfectionism That Drove Steve Jobs." The Atlantic. Atlantic Media Company, October 30, 2013. https://www.theatlantic.com/technology/archive/2011/11/crazy-perfectionism-drove-steve-jobs/335842/.

Ho-Jo. "Steve Jobs Biography." Encyclopedia of World Biography. Accessed August 27, 2021. https://www.notablebiographies.com/Ho-Jo/Jobs-Steve.html.

Investopedia. "What Is Tim Cook's Managerial Style?" Investopedia, August 2, 2021. https://www.investopedia.com/ask/answers/042315/what-apples-current-mission-statement-and-how-does-it-differ-steve-jobs-original-ideals.asp.

Jacobson, Brianna. "How Barbara Corcoran Went from a 2-Bedroom Flat to a Penthouse on Fifth Avenue." CNBC. CNBC, March 11, 2018. https://www.cnbc.com/2018/03/09/how-barbara-corcoran-went-from-a-2-bedroom-flat-to-a-penthouse-on-fifth-avenue.html.

Mikel, Betsy. "1 Personality Trait Steve Jobs Always Looked for When Hiring for Apple." Inc.com. Inc., December 11, 2017. https://www.inc.com/betsy-mikel/to-hire-all-star-employees-steve-jobs-looked-for-1-non-negotiable-quality.html.

Musil, Steven. "Execs Remember Steve Jobs as a Tireless Perfectionist." CNET. CNET, May 31, 2012. https://www.cnet.com/news/execs-remember-steve-jobs-as-a-tireless-perfectionist/.

CHAPTER 3

Loeffler, John. "The History Behind the Invention of the First Cell Phone." Interesting Engineering. Interesting Engineering, January 24, 2021. https://interestingengineering.com/the-history-behind-the-invention-of-the-first-cell-phone.

"Marty Cooper - The Father of the Cell Phone." Audible.com, December 21, 2020. https://www.audible.com/pd/Marty-Cooper-The-Father-of-the-Cell-Phone-Podcast/B08PJ123Z3.

Pichai, Sundar. "For the Next Five Billion: Android One." *Google* (blog). Google, September 15, 2014. https://blog.google/products/android/for-next-five-billion-android-one/.

Shiels, Maggie. "UK | A Chat with the Man Behind Mobiles." BBC News. BBC, April 21, 2003. http://news.bbc.co.uk/2/hi/uk_news/2963619.stm.

"Who Is Sundar Pichai, the New CEO of Both Google and Alphabet?" South China Morning Post, December 5, 2019. https://www.scmp.com/magazines/style/news-trends/article/3040719/who-sundar-pichai-millionaire-behind-google-chrome-and.

CHAPTER 4

"About SPANX Inc." Spanx.com. Accessed August 30, 2021. https://www.spanx.com/about-us.

CNET News. "When Jack Dorsey Speaks: 13 Notable Quotes." CNET. CNET, October 5, 2015. https://www.cnet.com/news/twitter-jack-dorsey-notable-quotes/.

Hof, Robert. "Uber-Entrepreneur Jack Dorsey to Startups: Don't Just Disrupt, Start a Revolution." Forbes. Forbes Magazine, September 10, 2012. https://www.forbes.com/sites/roberthof/2012/09/10/uber-entrepreneur-jack-dorsey-to-startups-dont-just-disrupt-start-a-revolution/?sh=5db97e2c13e2.

"How a Pitch in A Neiman Marcus Ladies Room Changed Sara BLAKELY'S LIFE." NPR. NPR, September 12, 2016. https://www.npr.org/transcripts/493312213.

Inc. "How Sara Blakely GOT Spanx Started." Inc.com. Inc., January 20, 2012. https://www.inc.com/sara-blakely/how-sara-blakley-started-spanx.html.

"Jack Dorsey." Biography.com. A&E Networks Television, May 18, 2021. https://www.biography.com/business-figure/jack-dorsey.

Jack Dorsey Quote: "The greatest lesson that I learned in all of this is that you have to start. Start now, start here, and start small. Kee...". Accessed August 30, 2021. https://quotefancy.com/quote/1166370/Jack-Dorsey-The-greatest-lesson-that-I-learned-in-all-of-this-is-that-you-have-to-start.

MasterClass. "All About Sara BLAKELY: Behind the SPANX FOUNDER'S Success - 2021." MasterClass. MasterClass, June 23, 2021. https://www.masterclass.com/articles/sara-blakely-founder-of-spanx#sara-blakelys-inspiration-for-spanx.

Moore, Thomas. "What's the Funniest Word in the World?" Babbel Magazine, February 4, 2021. https://www.babbel.com/en/magazine/whats-the-funniest-word-in-the-world.

CHAPTER 5

Estevez, Eric. "Warren Buffett: How He Does It." Investopedia. Investopedia, December 22, 2020. https://www.investopedia.com/ask/answers/081314/how-did-warren-buffett-get-started-business.asp#:~:text=%22What%20was%20the%20fee%20structure,%22%20Accessed%20March%206%2C%202020.

Hess, Abigail. "These Childhood Hobbies May Have Helped Warren Buffett Become a Billionaire." CNBC. CNBC, January 26, 2018. https://www.cnbc.com/2018/01/17/these-childhood-hobbies-may-have-helped-warren-buffett-become-a-billionaire.html.

"I Made My First Investment at Age Eleven. I Was Wasting My Life Up Until Then." Warren Buffett Quote. Accessed August 31, 2021. https://quotefancy.com/quote/931198/Warren-Buffett-I-made-my-first-investment-at-age-eleven-I-was-wasting-my-life-up-until.

"Inventright: How Did Stephen Get a Deal with Disney and Distribution with Walmart and 7-ELEVEN? With Stephen Key [SALES And Revenue]." INspired INsider - Inspirational Business Interviews with Successful Entrepreneurs and Founders with Dr. Jeremy Weisz. Accessed August 31, 2021. https://www.inspiredinsider.com/stephen-key-inventright-interview/.

Kennon, Joshua. "Warren Buffet: One of the Wealthiest People in America." The Balance, July 30, 2021. https://www.thebalance.com/warren-buffett-timeline-356439.

"Spinformation." InventRight. Accessed August 31, 2021. https://www.inventright.com/stephen-key-spinformation.

"Warren Buffett." Biography.com. A&E Networks Television, May 27, 2021. https://www.biography.com/business-figure/warren-buffett.

"Warren Buffett." Giving Pledge. Accessed August 31, 2021. https://givingpledge.org/Pledger.aspx?id=177.

"Why Did Warren Buffett Invest Heavily in Coca-Cola (KO) in the Late 1980S?" Investopedia. Investopedia, January 16, 2021. https://www.investopedia.com/ask/answers/021915/what-was-first-stock-warren-buffett-ever-bought.asp.

CHAPTER 6

Carlson, Nicholas. "JEFF BEZOS: Here's Why He Won." Business Insider. Business Insider, May 16, 2011. https://www.businessinsider.com/jeff-bezos-visionary-2011-4.

Carter, David. "In the Beginning There Was Amazon or 'Cadabra'?" Mogul Playground. Mogul Playground, September 16, 2020. https://www.mogulplayground.com/post/in-the-beginning-there-was-amazon-or-cadabra.

Cassell, Warren. "How Shark Tank's Robert Herjavec Made His Money." Investopedia. Investopedia, June 25, 2019. https://www.investopedia.com/articles/investing/101615/how-shark-tanks-robert-herjavec-made-his-money.asp.

Clifford, Cat. "3 Of Billionaire Jeff Bezos' Secrets to Success." CNBC. CNBC, July 5, 2019. https://www.cnbc.com/2019/07/05/amazon-turns-25-years-old-jeff-bezos-secrets-to-success.

Hamilton, Isobel Asher. "Jeff Bezos Is Stepping Down as Amazon's CEO. A Video of a Young Bezos from 1997 Shows Why He Decided to Build His Empire on Books." Business Insider. Business Insider, February 3, 2021. https://www.businessinsider.com/1997-jeff-bezos-amazon-empire-viral-video-books-2019-11.

Knapp, Alex. "Jeff Bezos' Space Plan: Building Infrastructure for the Next Generation." Forbes. Forbes Magazine, June 1, 2016. https://www.forbes.com/sites/alexknapp/2016/06/01/jeff-bezos-space-plan-building-infrastructure-for-the-next-generation/?sh=5127412f62b7.

Lagorio-Chafkin, Christine. "Shark Tank's Robert Herjavec: Accidental Entrepreneur to Master of Exits." Inc.com. Inc., June 11, 2012. https://www.inc.com/christine-lagorio/robert-herjavec-shark-tank-reluctant-entrepreneur.html.

Neate, Rupert. "Jeff Bezos: The Boy Who Wanted to Colonise Space." The Guardian. Guardian News and Media, April 25, 2018. https://www.theguardian.com/technology/2018/apr/25/jeff-bezos-the-boy-who-wanted-to-colonise-space.

"Robert Herjavec: Be Grateful for Life's Opportunities." Goalcast, May 5, 2017. https://www.goalcast.com/2017/05/05/robert-herjavec-be-grateful-lifes-opportunities/.

"Robert Herjavec Quotes." Quoteswise. Accessed September 4, 2021. http://www.quoteswise.com/robert-herjavec-quotes.html.

Smale, Thomas. "9 Quotes from the 'Shark Tank' Stars to Inspire You to Reach Your Goals." Entrepreneur, February 11, 2015. https://www.entrepreneur.com/article/242746.

CHAPTER 7

Bellis, Mary. "Biography of Mark Zuckerberg, Creator of Facebook." ThoughtCo, June 19, 2019. http://www.thoughtco.com/mark-zuckerberg-biography-1991135.

Ciotti, Gregory. "The Psychology of Getting More Done (in Less Time)." Entrepreneur. Entrepreneur, June 25, 2014. https://www.entrepreneur.com/article/234958.

"Hardest Countries to Immigrate to 2021." World Population Review. Accessed September 2, 2021. https://worldpopulationreview.com/country-rankings/hardest-countries-to-immigrate-to.

McFadden, Christopher. "A Brief History of Facebook, Its Major Milestones." Interesting Engineering. Interesting Engineering, July 7, 2020. https://interestingengineering.com/history-of-facebook.

"We're Stronger than We THINK: Interview with ASTRONAUT Jonny Kim '12." University of San Diego, December 11, 2020. https://www.sandiego.edu/news/detail.php?_focus=79328.

CHAPTER 8

"Dartmouth News." Dartmouth College. Accessed September 13, 2021. https://www.dartmouth.edu/press-releases/predisposed-tolearn073015.html.

Knyszewski, Jerome. "Ray Zinn of Micrel Semiconductor: 5 Things I Wish Someone Told Me Before I Began Leading My Company." Medium. Authority Magazine, February 21, 2021. https://medium.com/authority-magazine/ray-zinn-of-micrel-semiconductor-5-things-i-wish-someone-told-me-before-i-began-leading-my-company-4d2dd95fb911.

Robb, Alice. "The 'Flow State': Where Creative Work Thrives." BBC Worklife. BBC, February 5, 2019. https://www.bbc.com/worklife/article/20190204-how-to-find-your-flow-state-to-be-peak-creative.

"ZinnStarter." Carroll College, February 12, 2018. https://www.carroll.edu/article/zinnstarter.

CHAPTER 9

"3 Famous Billionaires and Their Mentors." Bcombinator. Accessed September 4, 2021. https://bcombinator.com/3-famous-billionaires-and-their-mentors.

Comaford, Christine. "76% of People Think Mentors Are Important, But Only 37% Have One." Forbes. Forbes Magazine, July 3, 2019. https://www.forbes.com/sites/christinecomaford/2019/07/03/new-study-76-of-people-think-mentors-are-important-but-only-37-have-one/?sh=78c1b4534329.

Cronin, Nicola. Mentoring Statistics: The Research You Need to Know, February 3, 2020. https://www.guider-ai.com/blog/mentoring-statistics-the-research-you-need-to-know.

CHAPTER 10

Stephanie. "Richard Branson: Billionaire Entrepreneur & Visionary." Talkroute, November 26, 2019. https://talkroute.com/richard-branson-billionaire-entrepreneur-visionary/.

CHAPTER 11

"About Lori - Lori Greiner: Inventor & Entrepreneur: Home." Lori Greiner: Inventor & Entrepreneur | Home. Accessed September 8, 2021. https://lorigreiner.com/about-lori/.

"About San Diego." SanDiego.com. Accessed September 8, 2021. https://www.sandiego.com/articles/2011-07-18/about-san-diego.

"Coming-Soon: Think and Grow Rich: The Legacy." Think and Grow Rich the Movie. Accessed September 8, 2021. https://members.thinkandgrowrich.shop/Coming-Soon.

Conner, Cheryl. "10 Top Keynote Speakers Tell How Presenting Advances Their PR Success." Forbes. Forbes Magazine, January 3, 2016. https://www.forbes.com/sites/cherylsnappconner/2016/01/03/10-top-keynote-speakers-tell-how-presenting-advances-their-pr-success/?sh=5f54204a394f.

Dolan, Eric W, and Antje Schmitt. Other. *A Good Action Plan Protects Your Goals from the Negative Impacts of Anger, Study Finds.* PsyPost, April 18. 2019. https://www.psypost.org/2019/04/a-good-action-plan-protects-your-goals-from-the-negative-impacts-of-anger-study-finds-53484.

Hochwald, Lambeth. "Lessons from the Shark Tank: Lori Greiner Shares Advice, Inspiration and a Season 9 Sneak Peek." Parade, September 15, 2017. https://parade.com/601966/lhochwald/lessons-from-the-shark-tank-lori-greiner-shares-advice-inspiration-and-a-season-9-sneak-peek/.

"Lori Greiner: Shark Tank." ABC. Accessed September 8, 2021. https://abc.com/shows/shark-tank/cast/lori-greiner.

"Meet the Sharks." CNBC. CNBC. Accessed September 8, 2021. https://www.cnbc.com/meet-the-sharks/.

Parker, Garrett. "20 Things You Didn't Know about LORI GREINER." Money Inc. Accessed September 8, 2021. https://moneyinc.com/10-things-didnt-know-lori-greiner/.

Robehmed, Natalie. "5 Lessons for Female Entrepreneurs from Shark TANK'S LORI GREINER." Forbes. Forbes Magazine, July 24, 2012. https://www.forbes.com/sites/natalierobehmed/2012/07/24/5-lessons-for-female-entrepreneurs-from-shark-tanks-lori-greiner/?sh=a9d746b4e517.

Roysam, Varsha. "15 Quotes from LORI Greiner That'll Wake the Entrepreneur in You." YourStory.com. Yourstory, December 19, 2016. https://yourstory.com/2016/12/inspirational-quotes-lori-greiner/amp.

Roysam, Varsha. "Lori Greiner: Tracing an Inventor's Entrepreneurial Journey and Achievements." YourStory.com. Yourstory, December 20, 2016. https://yourstory.com/2016/12/lori-greiner-journey-achievements/amp.

"Shark Tank Star Lori Greiner's 4 Money Rules for New Entrepreneurs." Yahoo! Yahoo! Accessed September 8, 2021. https://smallbusiness.yahoo.com/advisor/resource-center/shark-tank-star-lori-greiner-39-4-money-140000129/.

CHAPTER 12

"Dale Carnegie." Biography.com. A&E Networks Television, April 2, 2014. https://www.biography.com/writer/dale-carnegie.

Massan, Tara. "Study Finds Whether People with More Ambitious Goals Are Happier or Less Satisfied." Lifehack. Lifehack,

May 6, 2021. https://www.lifehack.org/403757/study-finds-people-with-ambitious-goals-are-happier-and-more-satisfied.

Morin, Amy. "5 Reasons Studies Say You Have to Choose Your Friends Wisely." Psychology Today. Psychology Today, April 10, 2015. https://www.psychologytoday.com/us/blog/what-mentally-strong-people-dont-do/201504/5-reasons-studies-say-you-have-choose-your-friends.

"The Most Entrepreneurial Ambitious Cities: A Global Index." How Entrepreneurial Is Your City? The Dojo Global Ambition Index." Dojo, April 28, 2021. https://dojo.tech/blog/most-entrepreneurial-ambitious-cities/.